AROUND THE ORKNEY PEAT-FIRES

AROUND THE ORKNEY PEAT-FIRES

NINTH EDITION

COMPILED BY

W. R. MACKINTOSH

Published by The Orcadian Limited, (Kirkwall Press),
Hell's Half Acre, Hatston, Kirkwall, Orkney

ISBN 1-902957-01-6

CONTENTS

⊰ — ⊱

Preface to the Ninth Edition

—⚞ —— ⚟—

"Around the Orkney Peat-Fires" first appeared in serial form in *The Orcadian* newspaper over one hundred years ago. It was highly popular with the readers and was later published as a book which has sold out many times.

W. R. Mackintosh, who compiled the book, came from Ayrshire. An accomplished journalist and shorthand-writer, he came to Orkney to work on *The Orcadian* and subsequently married Elizabeth Anderson, a daughter of the then owner. He eventually took over the business in 1895 and subsequently published a number of Orkney books.

The timeless *Around the Orkney Peat Fires* is regarded as a local "classic."

The ninth edition has been illustrated by Orcadian artist Jim Baikie, who is perhaps better known as a cartoonist, contributing to 'comics' around the world.

Kirkwall, July, 1999.

AROUND THE ORKNEY PEAT-FIRES

⊰⊱ —— ⊰⊱

INTRODUCTION

THE following tales, anecdotes and sketches are mostly, though not wholly, of a traditionary character. Prior to the days of cheap periodical literature, people were in the habit of gathering in neighbours' houses, and, seated round a rousing peat-fire, while away the long winter evenings recounting the achievements of notable Orcadians, telling of the eccentricities of local characters, describing all kinds of smuggling exploits, and relating many thrilling incidents connected with the press-gang. Before "the amers were raked" for the night, something creepy, generally in the shape of a witch story, was thrown in, so that the members of the company wended their way home in the dark, prepared to see a ghost in each waving thistle, or troops of fairies on every rising knoll.

The aim of this work is to reproduce these fireside tales in four parts. The first is devoted to smuggling anecdotes, the second gives tales of the press-gang, the third is mainly composed of witch and other stories, most of which are founded on fact and the last part deals with notable Orcadians.

PART I—SMUGGLING ANECDOTES

SMUGGLING TALES

It is probable that smuggling first commenced in Scotland about the latter part of the seventeenth century. At any rate, the first Excise Act was considered by the Scottish Parliament on 4th January, 1644, was dealt with in Committee on the 26th, and was passed on the 31st of the same month. It was ordered to be "furthwith printed and published at all the mercat crosses and parish kirkes of this kingdom q'throu nane pretend ignorance of the same." When first introduced, the Act specified a certain sum as due from each Scottish shire and burgh payable monthly.

In 1784 an Act (24 George III, c. 46) was passed, raising a charge upon the wash. It was doubtless felt that an attempt to enforce it in the Far North would render it a dead letter. For the Highlands, therefore, the measure made provision to charge the duties by means of annual licences. Section 45 of the Act declared that the Commissioners of Excise in Scotland might empower such persons as they thought proper to erect and work stills in producing spirits from corn, in Orkney, Caithness, and fifteen other counties. The heritors were required to assemble in the Parish Church in May, to make out a list of persons in each parish who were deemed fit and proper to be licensed to keep stills. The list was sent to the Excise Board at Edinburgh, and licences were issued in accordance therewith. Two persons were usually selected from each parish. The licence was 20s. per gallon of still content. This system continued down to 1804.

It may be mentioned that in Ireland a decree was issued in 1580, placing all illicit makers of *aqua vitae* under martial law—offenders to be hanged without delay. The officers had to make a monthly return of all who had been thus executed.

Shortly after the Scottish Excise Act came into force, smuggling was carried on very extensively in Orkney. The illicit traffic was not confined to the lower and middle classes. In fact these may be said to have merely done the drudgery work of the trade whilst the profits went into the pockets of the gentry.

Kirkwall was the headquarters of the smugglers in this county, and the wealthy merchants secured most of the profits. The Magistrates and Town Councillors took a leading part in the traffic, and it must be confessed that they carried on their operations with great success.

When excise officials arrived in the Burgh from the south, the Town Council always entertained them, and in this way they got much information of a valuable nature in regard to the plans laid for the capture of smuggled goods.

At that time smuggling was a business, and a very payable one to boot. People in town and country formed companies for running ships in the illicit trade just as they do in the present day for fishing. Public sympathy was entirely with the smugglers, and against the excisemen, so that it was a very rare thing for a contraband cargo to be seized.

Sometimes, of course, there were personal quarrels; and these occasionally resulted in a capture—information being given to the excise by one or other of the parties to the dispute.

It is not many decades since smuggled gin is said to have been disposed of quite publicly in a bank in town, and some heavy cargoes were landed in Kirkwall, which were disposed of to hotel-keepers and others.

Smuggling, however, is now a thing of the past. Farmers have got the privilege of brewing a little malt for themselves, and those who were in the habit of running cargoes of gin and whisky found that the trade had become a little too risky to be indulged in. Sometimes a Dutch lugger may dispose of a small cask of gin, or a parcel of tobacco to the crew of a local fishing boat, but the quality of these goods is generally so bad that the article would be dear at any money.

GEORGE EUNSON

George Eunson was a noted smuggler in his day. He was very clever, but was of a restless, roving disposition. He was apprenticed as a cooper, but the work was distasteful to him, and ultimately he went to sea.

He was a daring character, and just the sort of man that would make a successful smuggler. This was acknowledged on all hands, so that a company which had been formed to purchase a vessel for this illicit trade approached Eunson, and got him persuaded to take command of the ship.

Eunson, though clever in landing his cargoes, was not a success for his employers. He embezzled their goods, and made such exorbitant charges that they were glad to get rid of him.

Shortly after this, a privateer happened to come to Kirkwall and Eunson joined it. He seems to have been on it for a very short time, however, as the vessel was next heard of at Dunbar, where he was discharged.

Eunson then proceeded to Leith for the purpose of trying

to get a passage to Orkney, but he was captured by the press-gang, was put on board one of His Majesty's ships, was carried to the Nore, and fought against the Dutch. Subsequently his ship put into Sheerness for repairs; but by this time he had had enough of the Navy, so that he deserted, proceeded to London, and afterwards returned to Orkney.

Again he engaged in the smuggling trade, but, as formerly, he looked better after his own interests than those of his employers, so that he was once more dismissed.

About this time (1785), a great dispute arose over the election of the Right Hon. Charles James Fox. The Magistrates favoured the candidature of this eminent statesman, whilst the working classes, backed by Mr Baikie of Tankerness, supported Sir John Sinclair of Ulbster. Fox was ultimately elected, whereupon Mr Baikie and his friends proceeded to harass their opponents. George Eunson, through the influence of Mr Baikie, was appointed an officer of Excise; and, being an old smuggler, he was expected to know the business so well that high hopes were entertained he would be able to get the Magistrates convicted of participation in the forbidden traffic.

Eunson, however, lived a fast life, and his enemies were on the watch for him. One night he assaulted a shoemaker in Kirkwall and was apprehended for this crime. The Magistrates kept him in prison for ten weeks without a trial, and the usage he received was so bad that he sued them in the Sheriff Court for £200 damages. He lost this case, and afterwards raised an action in the Court of Session, concluding for £2000 damages against each of the Magistrates, and £100 for his own legal expenses.

In the petitions which were laid before the Courts in these actions, he gave the Magistrates a very bad character. He alleged that they were the chief smugglers in the town, and that he had been thrown into prison in revenge because he had tried to expose them.

In the year 1788 Eunson published a book at Newcastle, giving a short historical sketch of the county, and describing the state of the people. He spoiled his case, however, by the extravagance of his assertions; and, though he never mentions in the work the dispute he had with the Magistrates, the casual reader has no difficulty in arriving at the conclusion that in writing he is actuated strongly by a spirit of revenge.

The book, which is crown 8vo. in size, extends to 137 pages, and is now very rare, so that it realises at the present time from 16s. to 20s. It is entitled "The Ancient and Present State of Orkney. Particularly the Capital Borough of Kirkwall, to which are added, the Petty Tyrants, or Grinders of the Poor. The Characteristic New Year's Gift, or Lawrie's Elections. And lastly, Free National Thoughts upon Great Britain. The whole collected by G. Eunson, *Philo Patriae* 'Tell the Truth and Shame the Devil'—Proverbs."

In later years Eunson divided his time between smuggling and performing the duties of a North Sea pilot. When acting in the latter capacity on a man-of-war vessel, it went down with all hands.

Mansie o' Harra' and the Excisemen

In the days when illicit brewing was largely carried on in the county, Mansie o' Harra' was most successful in defrauding the Excise. He was, of course, suspected by the gaugers, but he was rather too knowing to be caught napping. It is told of Mansie, however, that he was prevailed upon to "enter his barm," and the next time he was to brew he sent a message to the gauger to come and measure his malt. The day was very stormy, and the exciseman endured great hardship on his journey. Mansie received the official blandly and after they had exchanged a few stories, the exciseman asked to be shown the malt that required to be measured. "Oh," replied Mansie, "we needna gang far tae see hid," and taking a mitten down from the roof, he handed it to the officer. Naturally, the exciseman was much exasperated at having had to travel such a long distance, and in such wild weather for the purpose of measuring a "mittenful" of malt; and he gave Mansie a dreadful scolding. "Weel, weel," coolly answered Mansie, "ye wanted tae ken whin I wis gaun tae brew, so that ye might measure me malt, and that was why I telt ye tae come." Seeing he was fairly hoaxed, the gauger left, vowing vengeance on poor Mansie. Some time after this, the exciseman again received intimation to measure Mansie's malt. On this occasion Mansie had a little more—having an old stocking filled and ready for his man. Again the gauger found himself duped, but Mansie loudly and vehemently maintained that he "Wisna tae bleem." Shortly afterwards Mansie again sent word to the exciseman that he had more malt, which he wished measured, but that official, thinking he was again to be hoaxed, returned the answer that he was not to come, and that his tormentor could brew all he had. "Aye, I thought as muckle," chuckled Mansie. "I wis sure I wid tire him oot." On this occasion it turned out that Mansie had some sackfuls, all of which he brewed free of any tax.

THE GAUGERS IN SHAPINSAY

Contraband liquor does not seem to have been produced in Shapinsay except for consumption by the party who made it, so the breaches of Excise law were of the mild sort. When milk was scant, or when a marriage was in prospect, a little ale was usually made; but it was for home use. There was no attempt to force exciseable liquor into the market. The excisemen, however, came from the south and prowled around the little homesteads, seeking for a paltry crown's worth of poor ale, which, even if it were sold, would not buy the dinner of the strangers. It was a case of burning a penny candle to search for a lost farthing.

The excisemen usually travelled by boat from Kirkwall and landed at Sound, on the south end of the island. On one occasion, after trudging and searching over eight miles, they made a seizure—a small one—at Holm. The liquor was confiscated, and the owners cited and fined. The excisemen were jubilant over the conviction. But it does not appear that such prosecutions had any effect save to make the parties concerned fix upon a securer hiding place for the next brewing. On another occasion the search-party discovered some liquor at the house of a man named Nicolson, in the Sands district, Then followed the usual judgment and fine.

But one day the excisemen made rather an unexpected, extraordinary, and startling find. Immediately on landing, a company of the more stalwart islanders met them, and intimated that they must take an idle day; that they would not be allowed to search any house on the isle. The officers would not, or could not, persuade themselves that such an intimation was seriously meant, but the defence party quickly gave them to understand that no excise business would be done in the isle; and the excisemen had perforce to return whence they came. The gaugers did not take this repulse in good part, for they seem to have said to themselves, "Well, if we can't get the liquor and the fine, at least we can get the people who made it." So half a dozen Shapinsay men spent that winter in Kirkwall, being boarded and lodged at the Government's expense—in prison.

A most notable instance of a woman's pluck occurred at the North End of the island. The excisemen had quietly landed at the west side of the North Point, and were at the door of the house in question before any notice was received of their presence—at least there was not a moment in which to conceal anything effectually. A sack of malt was lying on the kitchen floor, and not a man was in the house. The guidwife, however, was equal to the occasion. She seized the dangerous bag, threw it in the box-bed, shut the doors, and put her back to them. The officers came in, looked around, told her to move till they glanced into the bed; but she remained firm. All their persuasion could not make the woman budge from the bed door. They were obliged to move on and search elsewhere—and, it is needless to say, they did so in vain.

Again they landed at the North End before there was time to conceal anything. As they drew near to the house above referred to, one of the officers espied a man stealing away from the rear of the house bearing a sack on his back; and he (the officer) started off in pursuit. The man with the sack hurried along a very narrow path that winds round southwards among the cliffs. Suddenly he dropped his burden through an aperture in the rocks into the darkness of a cave. But the officer saw the movement, and hurried to the spot. It was evident, however, that no human being could venture through that forbidding crevice. But he was a determined man. Making his way down the face of the cliffs, he began examining, and at length found the seaward and only passable path into the cave. Subsequently he discovered the sack of malt which he had so much coveted, not for its money, but for its evidential value. But what to do with it was the puzzle. To lug it up the rocks and along the tortuous path by which he had descended, was a hopeless task; and to leave it for the purpose of sending for help would be equally vain, as he knew right well the sack would not be suffered to lie there till he should return. So at last he hit upon a means of at least spoiling the malt. He dragged the sack up to the grassy banks above and ripped it from end to end, scattering its contents as far as possible.

A very serious affray happened at the Sands and East District of the island. Rather a strong force of excisemen had landed there, and were proceeding as usual to search house after house, when they were met by a stronger force of the natives; there were hard knocks going, and the officers were obliged to withdraw. Later on, the names of some, if not all, of the opposing Shapinsay men were obtained and warrants issued; and after trial and conviction, they were taken to Edinburgh prison. The sentence was a severe one, for some of the men, as it seems, were detained in prison for eighteen months, and even then were liberated under special favour in response to the earnest intercession of Mr Laing, then M.P. for the County. Among those sent the Edinburgh jail was one man of such size that he could not be fitted with the very biggest prison suit. After trying to get their prisoner covered in the best manner possible, the officials consoled themselves by saying, "If we cannot make the clothes fit the prisoner, we'll make the prisoner fit the clothes." And we have no doubt that the scant fare soon made the big prisoner small enough.

RUNNING AN ILLICIT CARGO IN ROUSAY

In the early part of last century smuggling was not considered any crime. As we have already indicated, boats were fitted up, and regularly manned, to carry on the illicit traffic between

Orkney and Shetland and other places. At the northwest side of Northmavine, Shetland, there is a voe into which, in those days, Orkney boats used to go to load up. One of these vessels had arrived from Shetland, and was in the act of unloading somewhere below Banks, Sourin, Rousay, when intelligence was received that the authorities at Kirkwall were on the alert. The smugglers thereupon posted a sentinel in proper position to watch for the appearance of the Customs officers. Meanwhile a boat was manned with the ablest fellows that could be found in Rousay, fishing tackle was shipped and every preparation made for putting to sea. Soon afterwards the sentinel gave the signal that the Customs boat was approaching. Whenever the officials came in sight, the Rousay crew bent to their oars, and pulled for all they were able out through Lengantong. The officers, thinking the smuggled goods would be on board, at once went in pursuit. An exciting chase ensued, till the Rousay boatmen were far out in the Westray Firth, when they quietly laid in their oars, put out their lines and commenced to fish. Their pursuers on coming alongside were chagrined to find that their labour had all been in vain. They hurried back, but when they rounded the Head of Faraclett, and were off Scockness, the ebb tide had set in so strong that it was impossible to get in to Sourin. After several vain attempts at either side of the holm, they had to lie-to till the tide turned— some five or six hours. By that time the people on shore had managed to stow away the contraband goods, so that the officers had to return to Kirkwall defeated and discouraged.

HOW AN EXCISEMAN WAS OUTWITTED

Not many generations ago there was a very vigilant officer appointed for Orkney, who became quite a terror to the community of malt-makers. He was here, there, and everywhere, No recess or "hidie-hole" seemed secure from his professional instinct. He was a stout fellow and an athlete. Personal violence in defence of the treasured goods was rarely thought of in Orkney, but cunning and ready wit often came in handy.

In smuggling times two peaceful, law-abiding loyal subjects might have been seen in one of the South Isles taking an early constitutional along the banks—one a tall muscular fellow with a telescope under his arm, the other just a farmer body. As they rounded a point and came into full view of the Pentland the former stopped, levelled his glass, and exclaimed, "John, see you that boat heading straight for the haven of B——. I bet you a guinea that's some of the S—— villains again. If there's not something for me in yon craft, I'm a goose. Lie down, man, and I'll nab them, sure as my name's McC——."

The unsuspecting yawl was rapidly drawing near, and McC—— was all alive with expectation, when his companion gave a groan and cried, "Man, McC——, are ye never troubled wi' a pain in your stomach. Sic a rumblin' is in ma inside enoo!"

"No, no, I'm as sound inside and out as a horse."

Another groan followed, and the farmer continued, "I'm no' had ony peace to speak o' since I had pork and kail and tatties to ma dinner yesterday. Man it's a gran' feed, but a body pays weel for't." The farmer was apparently so ill he could not walk, and the exciseman rounded the point alone. A few minutes afterwards, however, John rejoined his companion, quite relieved, and seemingly at peace with all mankind.

McC—— by this time was so intent watching his prey that he paid no heed to the farmer, but stood gazing at the small boat, which kept on its course till just in front of the landing-place, when down went the helm and 'bout ship, and the gallant little craft was reeling northwards with the strong ebb under her lee bow.

"Man! ever saw ye anything so galling as that?" exclaimed the exciseman, stamping like a lunatic and imprecating like a fiend. "They were running slap into my claws, and now see where they are."

"Peace, man, peace," replied the farmer, "Ye'll mak' the rock fa'. Dae ye no ken, wi' the wind as it is, they maun tack and tack, first to this lan' then to that? They're gaun to the mill o' Rysa wae a puckle burstin', ye'll see."

"D——l burst them," retorted the exciseman, "come away; I'll nick them yet."

What code of signals was used by the farmer do not transpire; but it is pretty clear they were understood by those in the boat, from the clever way they put their craft about.

AN ATHLETIC FEAT

It was in the "voar" (spring) time, when ploughing on the small farms was in full swing, with peat-cutting approaching, and consequently a drink of ale was much needed. The cottars therefore began to brew on a small scale.

"A stane or twa o' maut, man, what's it? A drink o' ale hurts naebody, far less the Queen. Never tell me she's fashin' her thoom aboot us or it! Na, man, it's that thief McC——, the ragin', rampagin' lion! An' certie, if that's no him comin' swinging wi' his stick, as sure as I'm a sinner. Here am I atween the stilts o' this auld pleugh. What's to be dune? I have a kirn o' wirt, and the barm just beginning to work. I maun lowse the pleugh and spill it in the gutter powe!"

"Wheesht, man, yer a fool! Pleugh awa'. If he saw ye gang into th' hoose he'd smell a rat, an' be on ye in a crack. He's gleg i' the een is McC——."

This conversation took place between a crofter and his next neighbour, who had the licence to sell a dram. "But," continued the crofter, "he'll be in at the wife in a jiffy, an' we'll be ruined."

"Ye canna help yersel', Johnnie. Risk it. I'll see if I canna come ower him some gate."

By this time the "Lion" was coming up the brae at a good round pace. Of course Brooks, the licensed dealer, was well known to him, and they often had a passage-at-arms. So Brooks turned and began the play.

"Hoo's a' wi ye this morning McC——? Yer early astir th' day; but, man, I'm sorry to see ye looking sae ill, and yer puffin' like a palluck. I doot yer on yer last legs McC——."

"Toots, man," replied the gauger, "I'm as sound as a bell."

"May be," pawkily put in Brooks; "but ye ken some bells are crack't."

"Ha, ha!" laughed the exciseman; "I canna help it. I maun hae a shot when I see a chance."

"But look here," said Brooks, "if you're in sic guid trim, and as ye aye blaw sae muckle o' yer leaping, I'll wager ye a bottle o' my best whisky ye winna spring clear ower th' back o' this bit pownie o' Johnnie's here!"

"Done!" cried the gauger; "I accept your bet." Then addressing the crofter, he continued, "Turn your pony man. There, hold his head." Going a few steps backwards, the doughty exciseman at once made a big flying leap, clearing the ridge bone of the animal with something to spare.

"Fool fa' that! I didna think ye had steel springs in ye," grumbled Brooks. "Never mind; come awa' an' taste yer earnings; and ye, Johnnie, when ye stable an' feed yer beasties, come ower th' gate an' help us."

So saying, Brooks hooked his hand in the exciseman's arm, leaving Johnnie to stow away his pickle ale in peace, and then join his friends in demolishing the gauger's bottle of whisky. If they sat till fou', and till the bottle was empty, tradition sayeth not; but Johnnie's malt paid no duty that time.

MYSTIFICATION OF TWO EXCISEMEN

In smuggling times two excisemen might have been seen walking along the Yesnabie district in Sandwick. Pointing to a croft close to the banks, one of the excisemen gave it as his opinion that it was the house of Lee, and if so, from the information he had received, he was sure they would find a quantity of malt there. They made straight for the house, but were met at the door by two stalwart women.

"I suppose," said one of the excisemen, "you will have no objection to our inspecting your house."

"Weel," replied the elder of the two women, "there are no men folk in the hoose jist noo, an' ye being strangers, hid widna be very safe to lat you in."

"We are excisemen," continued the stranger, "and we are bound to get in."

"Try to enter this door," exclaimed the woman brandishing

a bismar in the face of the exciseman, "an I'll bane-briss the pair o' ye!"

The woman seemed so determined and courageous, that the excisemen drew back a few paces and held a consultation. The spokesman then advised the women to let them make a peaceable inspection of the house, otherwise they would be severely punished.

"Hae ye a warrant for forcin' yirsels into law-abiding folks' houses?" demanded the angry woman.

"We have not," admitted the exciseman, "but my friend here will go and get one from a Justice of the Peace, and meantime, I will keep guard at the door to see that no malt leaves the premises."

"Git yir warrant," snapped the woman, "an' then we'll see whit can be dune," and so saying, she slammed the door in the faces of the officers.

The exciseman had two miles to tramp before he reached the residence of the Justice of Peace, so that a long time elapsed before he returned. When he and his companion at length approached the house of Lee, armed with their warrant, they were quite surprised at the kindly reception they received.

"Come awa' ben, gentlemen," said one of the women. "we are sorry to hae keepit ye waitin' sae lang, but law's law, an' it wis only right that ye should hae a warrant, ye ken."

The excisemen at once began the search, but, needless to say, they discovered no malt. However, there were sufficient indication to show that it had been removed very shortly before, but how this could have been done was a mystery to the gaugers. And yet the whole thing was simple enough.

The men belonging to the house were at sea, close by, and during the time the exciseman was away getting the warrant, one of the women left the premises by a back door, ran to the crags and signalled her friends to come ashore, which they at once did. They quietly removed a flag from the roof of the room where the malt was, put the stuff in bags, and quickly transferred it. Thus in a very short time they had the whole contraband down at the shore beyond the reach of the excise officers. Of course the house was so situated on the banks that the unsuspecting excisemen could not see what was going on.

TWO SACKS OF MALT

The people in the township of Northdyke, Sandwick, were busy brewing one spring, in preparation for their peat-cutting, when some excise officers appeared in the district. Entering a chaumer—a room at a few yards' distance from a dwelling-house—occupied by William Smith, they found two sacks filled with malt. Naturally enough, the gaugers charged the party who occupied the adjoining dwellinghouse with ownership of the malt. But nobody in the township would admit of it being theirs. There were letters on the sacks, but these were not sufficient to lead to the identification of any particular person. At length the exisemen sent to Skaill for a cart, in which the malt was conveyed to Stromness. No buyer, however, could be found for it. The real owner of the malt put on a bold front to the excisemen, and pretended to help them with his advice, so that suspicion never once lighted on him. So busy were the gaugers kept over these two sacks of malt, too, that all the other people in the district got plenty of time to put their brewings out of sight, and there were no prosecutions at that time—the excisemen having all their trouble for nothing.

A WOMAN'S PRACTICAL JOKE

On one occasion two excisemen, when in the Housegar district, Sandwick, saw a woman rushing up past the farm steading of Bain, carrying a sack on her back. They at once gave chase. The woman, seeing this, made direct for a loch close by. In this loch there were a number of holms, which could only be reached by wading through the water. The woman plunged through the loch, and landed her burden on one of the holms. One of the gaugers, more courageous than the other, at the expense of wet garments, followed the woman through the loch, and succeeded in capturing both her and the sack. When he opened it, however, his disgust may be

imagined when he found it was filled with chaff! A number
of people who were in the plot followed up the gaugers and
greatly enjoyed the fun.

AN UNSUCCESSFUL TRIP

In the days when smuggling was largely carried on in Orkney,
Stroma on account of its isolation became a favourite
rendezvous for landing illicit cargoes. On one occasion the
excise officers learned of a large quantity of "stuff" having
been stored on that island and immediately proceeded to
Scapa with a view to hiring a boat and proceeding to Stroma
in search of the smuggled goods. On reaching Scapa they
intimated to the boatman, S——, that they wished to get to
St Margaret's Hope without delay, and offered a high fare
if he would start as soon as possible. A bargain was struck
immediately, and the boat started. When well out Scapa
Flow, the excise officers told the boatman that they had no
intention of going to St Margaret's Hope, but that he would
have to land them on Stroma. "Na, na," replied S——, "I
was freighted to go to the Hope, and if ye dinna want to go
there, we jist can go back again." This, of course, would
not suit the officers, so they demurely assented to proceed.
When nearing Holm Sound the excisemen again
endeavoured to get S—— to land them in Stroma, and on
his refusal, attempted to take charge of the boat themselves,
but S——, fairly aroused, lifted the helm and swore that
the first man who tried to take the "tiller" from him, he
"wid knock his brains oot." In due course then, the boat
reached St Margaret's Hope, when the gaugers immediately
hired a South Ronaldsay crew to row them to Stroma. S——,
knowing their errand, and being aware that the Stroma men
were ignorant of the excise officers' proximity, asked the
South Ronaldsay boatmen to be as slow in their preparations
as possible, so as to enable him to get the alarm sent to
Stroma. A man on horseback was quietly dispatched to the
South Parish with the news of the officer's intentions, and
on the information becoming known, a boat was

immediately launched and rowed with all haste to Stroma,
where the alarm was given. So well had S—— played his
part, that long before the excisemen reached Stroma
everything in the shape of contraband goods was safely
hidden away. On the officers landing, they at once became
a "but of ridicule" for the islanders. Nothing daunted,
however, they commenced their fruitless search; and at last
were compelled to quit the island thoroughly discomfited
and chagrined at the neat way they had been over-reached
by their boatman.

A WOMAN'S WIT

A little ale was much more in demand in the Mainland some fifty years ago than even at the present day; and one worthy, a small farmer, had dared to get a little malt manufactured and ready for the "quern." The stuff was standing behind the fire in two handy baskets.

For the benefit of those who don't know better, it may be explained that these baskets were made of straw and "floss" bands, much in the form of an Indian's canoe. A basket of this description had a handle at each end, and was laced together at the top. In the house where the following incident took place, the fire was built close up to a small bit of stone wall, about three feet high, standing in the middle of the room. Those were the days of large fires, and as a result, plenty of "reek" and "ase"—sandy or surface peats being largely used for keeping up the heat. The ashes were pushed behind the "back," or fire wall, through a hole at the bottom left for this purpose. When a good heap had accumulated, it was transferred to the byre as bedding, and is said to have formed a valuable manure.

This was the condition of things when the guidman came hurrying into the house and exclaimed, "Lass, what's to be done? Here's the gauger, an' the grain o' maut standin' there in a great swither."

"Deed, Patie," answered the guidwife, "I telt thee to get it awa' 'but.' Hooever, ane micht as weel speak to the stane wa', th'u are sic na slither." The guidwife was making breakfast pottage whilst this conversation was going on, and it will be readily inferred that in this case, at least, the "grey mare seems to have been the better horse."

"Whaur is he, man?" she continued. "Is he faur aff?"

"Na," answered her husband, "he'll be here in twa meenits."

"Weel, stan' na' gapin' there," cried the guidwife, "but tak' thee to this," handing him the pot. "Stick thee nose in the pot and keep her there. Lay thee at it an' sup for a' that th'u are worth. Lift no thee heid for the life o' thee, for if he sees thee face he'll ken fine th'ure feart. Rise no', or th'us get it on the croon wi' this," brandishing a wooden implement used for shovelling off the ashes.

The house was pretty full of smoke, and to add to the obscurity she began working among the ashes, filling up one "keshie" and smacking it well down, which raised such a fog that one could scarce breathe. This one finished, she began to the other, shovelling in ashes on the top of the malt. It was scarcely covered when in stepped the exciseman.

"P——f! preserve us all! What's this?" he exclaimed, and backed off a bit, trying to recover his breath.

"O whane! O whane! Mr ——, is that you? Sic a mess for a gentleman to come into. I'm jist clearin' oot this ase; it's lyin' here till it's nearly gaun ower us. Jist wait a wee till I get it into the byre to bed the kye, and this funk clears a bit. Then ye can come in an' ransal an' hunt to your heart's content. Never a thing's here, as ye'll see. I'm grieved to keep you standing there." Then turning to her husband, she exclaimed, "Patie, ye villain, sit na there fillin' thee a' day, but come an' git this 'ase' ower to the byre, so that we can offer the gentleman a comfortable seat."

Patie, crouching low, obeyed, and each taking a handle, lugged the "asie keshies" away into the byre (the communication being by a door between kitchen and byre). By the time all this was accomplished, the dust had considerably subsided and the gauger was able to begin his search. Completely thrown off the scent by a woman's ready wit, it is needless to say that he found nothing, and the malt was none the worse after being winnowed and thereby freed of the dust.

A WARM RECEPTION

Excise officers were often the victims of practical jokes. On one occasion two gaugers went to the farm of Howe, in Sanday, to have a hunt for malt. Meeting one of the servants near the kiln, they asked what was on it. They were told that it was black oats that were being dried. They did not believe this statement, and proceeded to the place to have a look for their own satisfaction. The servant quietly followed them and fastened the door from the outside. After ranging all over the kiln and finding nothing there but black oats, they tried to get out, but discovered that they had been locked in. As the smoke in the place was momentarily getting more dense and the heat equal almost to a furnace, they began to get alarmed and shouted for assistance. It was a long time before their cries were heard, and when at length they were released by the tenant of the farm (a Mr Thomson), they were in a sorry plight. Mr Thomson asked for an explanation, and when he had got it, he expressed the opinion that their punishment was not altogether undeserved, seeing that they had refused to accept the word of his servant. At length he took them into the house and gave them any amount of whisky to drink, and succeeded in getting rid of them in the best of spirits. They had been so upset at being locked up in the stifling atmosphere of the kiln that they had not the heart to prosecute their search in other parts of the farm, so that they lost a splendid chance of having their revenge. At the time of their visit there was a very large quantity of malt lying in the barn, and if they had gone there they could not have failed to have discovered it.

A Painful Incident

Sometimes when the excisemen made a raid in the islands they were accompanied by a number of assistants, known as rangers. Both excisemen and rangers were of course hated by the people. And there were reasons for this. When they entered a house they overturned everything in their search, and as they never put matters right before leaving a farm, the occupants had generally to spend hours in restoring articles to their proper place. On one occasion a boat containing a number of men was seen making for North Ronaldsay. A crowd of spectators gathered along the shore to await the arrival of the supposed gaugers and rangers. When the boat was quite close to the island, however, it was struck by a sudden squall and overturned. If the natives of North Ronaldsay had cared to put off to the rescue, there is no doubt they could have saved many, if not most, of the men; but they had such a hatred of the gaugers that they stood and watched the whole of the occupants of the boat drowning, without offering a helping hand. It afterwards transpired that the unfortunate men were cattle-dealers who were on a passage to North Ronaldsay for the purpose of trying to purchase horses and cattle.

GRATITUDE OF AN EXCISEMAN

As still further illustrating the bad feeling of Orcadians towards excisemen, another case may be cited. One winter day an officer, located at Stromness, started for a search in the districts of Ireland, Orphir and Stenness. He was riding a horse, and the poor brute got quite exhausted for want of food. The exciseman tried farmer after farmer for a feed of oats for his nag, but was always refused. About seven o'clock at night, when in a lonely part of Stenness, he saw a light in a window, and resolved to make one more trial for provender for his animal. When he went up to this house the farmer was busy making a large quantity of malt. The exciseman asked for food for his horse; and as the old farmer saw he was in a scrape he at once complied with the request. He also invited the gauger to go into the dwellinghouse and get some refreshments for himself. The officer, however, possibly suspecting that the old farmer was in agony at the prospect of being captured, elected to remain where he was while his horse was being fed. He produced a flask of whisky, gave the farmer a drink of it, and sat and talked to him for a couple of hours. At length he took his departure without choosing to notice the malt, the fumes of which penetrated the whole buildings. The farmer shrewdly suspected the exciseman knew what was going on, but declined to be inquisitive owing to the kindness he had received. As the fine exactable would have ruined him, the farmer got such a fright that he made up his mind he should never again engage in the illicit traffic.

AN EXCITING RUN

A story is told in Birsay of a Swannay man who was trudging along the road one day with a keg of gin on his back, which he had stowed away in an old caisie. All at once a gauger hove in sight and, suspecting he had got a victim, set off in pursuit. There is an old saying—malicious, of course, and without the shadow of a shade of truth in it—that a Birsay man could be known anywhere in Orkney by this sign, that if there was a dyke near at hand he was sure to be leaning on it! This Swannay man, however, had no time to rest himself upon a wall. He had to decide on the spur of the moment how he could best save himself, his keg and his caisie from the enemy. He tore along through the peat-banks and hollows of Risdae, at the south-west end of Costa Hill, the gauger being in hot pursuit. After dodging out and in through the peat-banks, he made straight for the high sea cliffs, swung the caisie off his back and cast it into the surging waters beneath. The gauger thus had his race for nothing; but he went home happy in the belief that the smuggled drink was also destroyed. The Birsay man knew better, however, and after he got rid of the exciseman he returned to Risdae and secured his keg. When running among the peat-banks there he had given a dexterous hitch to his caisie, throwing the keg into the bottom of one of the holes. The exciseman did not notice the trick, and the Swannay man therefore retained the keg with its contents.

A MIDNIGHT SEARCH

When a man named George Mowat was in Overbist, Birsay, the rangers paid him a midnight visit. They came from Evie, but a runner sent from that district arrived before them, to give warning of their approach. Farmer George just had time to secret his kegs under the blankets beside his bairns when the excise officers arrived.

Apparently everybody was then asleep and had no idea of their danger. When at last the excisemen got entrance to the house, the kegs were "not at home" to such visitors. The blankets kept their own counsel, for if the officers had been so rude as to interfere with the bairns in bed, George would have made short work of them, being a strong man and a fierce. The officers thus had to retire from Overbist discomfited, and the kegs were shortly afterwards put beyond all danger.

Two Fat Grice

There is a tradition in the West Mainland to the effect that the Customs' officials were in the habit of giving a quiet word of warning to the country people before the raid of the rangers commenced, so that malt and smuggled spirits could be put in a place of safety. It is also stated that these Government officials received yearly a nice keg of gin, stowed away in a sack of "scrubs," as an acknowledgment of their kindly help in time of need. One day the rangers arrived at Aikerness in Evie, but the proprietor got a hint that they were coming, and met them outside, having previously placed two kegs of Holland in an outhouse, the door of which he left open. As the officials passed each door, they asked what was in the various houses. When they arrived at the place where the kegs were hidden, they put the question, "And what have you in this house?" "Twa fat grice," was the reply; "come awa' in an' see them." Being so freely invited to enter the pig-house, the officers jumped to the conclusion that there could not be anything of a suspicious character in it, and so they declined the invitation. Subsequently they went into the dwellinghouse and partook of the laird's hospitality, after which they inquired for places where they would be likely to find smuggled gin. The laird was anxious to get rid of them and directed them to the most unlikely spot in the whole parish—the Mill of Costa. The rangers went there, but it need scarcely be added that they did not get what they wanted.

A Race for Nothing

One day two excisemen visited the island of Graemsay for the purpose of searching for malt. A native of that island, who was reputed to be somewhat of a fool, noticed the approach of the two strangers; and, knowing that some malt was being made in the vicinity, gave the signal, and then set off at a run towards the other side of the island, the wind being right in his teeth. The excisemen seeing this, and noticing that the man had a caisie on his back, started off in pursuit. After a long hunt, the supposed fool turned and faced his pursuers, throwing the chaff and dust with which the caisie was filled right into the faces of the gaugers. By this time the malt was hidden, and the excisemen, after being so neatly tricked, left the island without visiting a single house.

A Farmer's Ruse

Sometimes the Excise officers were cheated in a very simple way. A farmer in Westray got word that the rangers were approaching his house. He was satisfied that he had no time to get the malt he was working at put into a satisfactory hiding-place, so he pulled it in front of the barn door, covered it up with grain, and began winnowing. When the excisemen entered the barn, and saw the chaff being driven out at the opposite door as was customary when winnowing in those days, they departed to other parts of the farm in search of the malt which was lying under their very noses. The farmer who played this trick off so successfully became quite a hero in the eyes of his neighbours.

An Angry Farmer

A farmer in Finya, Harray, had just taken his malt out of steep one day, when two excisemen paid him an unexpected and unwelcome visit. The old man was taken by surprise, so that he had not time to put the malt out of the way. The excisemen, as was usual on such occasions, ordered the grain to be taken out to the midden and destroyed. As this process was being carried on, the owner lost his temper and attacked the gaugers with the tongue. He seemed more concerned about the loss of his ale than the punishment which assuredly awaited him for smuggling. Addressing the excisemen, he shouted, "Deil tak' the pair o' ye for destroying me 'aere' o' guid ma't. Hid wad hae gi'en me mony a guid drink; but noo I'll hae tae sit wi' a dry moo for mony a day!"

A Narrow Escape

The following is very likely a story which has already been told, but as it comes from a different correspondent, it may be reproduced: There was a family at Yesnabie in Sandwick in the smuggling days who both brewed ale and distilled whisky, which was rather unusual in Orkney. The rangers had evidently received a hint of this fact, and one day they paid a visit to the house when the father and two sons were off at the sea. It so happened that a quantity of whisky had been distilled the previous day, and a large quantity of malt was at that very moment laid out in a back room, being got ready for another "brew." When the rangers entered the house, one of them made at once for this room. The good lady in charge, however, disputed his right to enter it, which so exasperated the excise officer that he gave her a slap on the face. In self-defence the woman lifted the tongs and thrashed the officers out of the house. A neighbour who noticed what was going on, ran down to the beach and signalled to the father and sons that they were wanted immediately. The men hurried ashore, rushed up to the house and dared the excisemen to enter the place. One of the officers, looking to the serious aspect which affairs had then assumed, hurried off to Skaill to get a warrant from the laird, who was a Justice of the Peace. Meantime, one of the sons of the house got into a wrangle with the remaining officer at the front door, which was kept up till the Justice of Peace arrived with the warrant. The door

was then opened, when the mistress of the house explained
that she had no desire to prevent a search of the premises being
made, but that the rangers had brought the trouble upon
themselves by their own impertinence and by having struck
her. Without parley, a search was made all over the farm, but
neither whisky, ale nor malt was found; and the Justice of the
Peace in the circumstances recommended the officers to take
no notice of the treatment they had received, seeing they had
been the aggressors. The house where this fracas took place was
quite close to the cliffs at Sandwick, and whilst the one son
was engaging the attention of the exciseman, the other, with
the assistance of his father and some neighbours, had filled
the malt and spirits into sacks, had removed one of the large
flags from the back portion of the roof, and slipped over to
the cliffs with them, dropping them down into Humlagoe.

A NOTED SMUGGLER

Captain A—— was a noted smuggler in Orkney many years
ago. He was a native of Hull, but he formed a connection
in Orkney, where he did a big trade in contraband goods. The
plan he adopted was to take a cargo of spirits out of bond at
Leith, carry it to Faroe, discharge it there, and then bring it
to Orkney with dried fish and Faroe cattle and ponies. To land
the smuggled spirits at some of the outlying islands was a
comparatively easy task at that time, but to take them to
Kirkwall was a more daring proceeding. However, the Captain
was equal to the undertaking. His friends were always on the
look-out for him, and on arriving off Deerness he at once gave
the signal when he would come in. About midnight he usually
worked his vessel up the String without showing a light, would
sail into Kirkwall, discharge his cargo, then go out till next
morning, when he returned as if he had just arrived from
Faroe.

He carried on the business for a long time without mishap,
but a capture came at last. He had landed a cargo in the manner
described, coming from Westray direction, and a porter was
sent off to watch the house of an exciseman to see when he

went to bed. This official had probably come to know the smuggler's plans, for about midnight he extinguished his light, and those engaged to work the cargo then began to deliver the casks to the purchasers. When the exciseman went out on the search he had little difficulty in getting hold of at least a portion of the spirits. He found one party sitting on a cask helplessly drunk, singing "Rule Britannia," and in a shed in Castle Street he discovered another three or four casks.

Those connected with this case were so heavily fined that there seemed to be little desire on the part of the culprits to engage in the trade again.

On one occasion, Captain A—— carried a cargo of smuggled goods to Stromness, left his vessel there, and proceeded to Kirkwall to look for customers. Meantime, the Custom House officers had got a hint of what was going on, and resolved to capture the spirits before they were landed. The smuggler was standing drinking at the bar of one of the Kirkwall hotels when he was told the Custom officers were to leave for Stromness next morning. "Let them go," he exclaimed with a laugh; "they will be welcome to all they find." Then turning to the landlord he ordered a bed for the night. Later on he privately gave orders for a hire to Stromness. Arriving there, he at once got his cargo discharged and hidden. After breakfast he set out for Kirkwall again, and was delighted to meet the officers at Finstown on their way westward, and it is needless to say they had their trouble for nothing. They were so angry because of their raid being unsuccessful that they placed an officer in charge of the vessel. Some days afterwards, when A—— went back to his ship and found an officer there he was somewhat nettled. "What depth of water have we here?" demanded A——. The officer replied that he did not know. "Very well," continued the smuggler, "if you do not get off my ship within the next five minutes I will send you down to measure the depth." As the officer had no desire to keep company with the crabs he speedily stepped ashore, and the smuggler weighed anchor for Faroe.

Captain A—— had a very narrow escape in landing his last cargo in Orkney. He suspected that one of his crew was not to be depended upon, and he kept him in the hold as the vessel was approaching the Orkney Islands. The spirits were landed at one of the South Isles, and this was duly reported to the authorities; but their informant could only state that there were large hills at the place where the kegs were discharged. Acting on this hint, the coastguard went off in search; but they were a little late, for by the time they reached the spot where the kegs had been hidden the contraband goods had been transferred elsewhere.

After this, Captain A—— arrived at the conclusion that smuggling was not a payable business, because he saw there was not only the risk of being caught, but also the chance of losing money, as his customers did not always pay up as they might have done. Having thus got disgusted with the trade he went to Australia, where he is said to have got an appointment in the Customs, and his former experience in this country would no doubt be of value to him in his new home in the detection of smugglers.

MANSIE EUNSON, A KIRKWALL SMUGGLER

This noted smuggler was was no relation of George Eunson, but he was better known to a former generation. He was flesher, beadle, and a successful smuggler. In addition to this, he was a born character, brimful of pawky humour and resource, which extricated him from many a scrape.

One day he was walking along the St Andrews road when he met Mr Baikie, the laird of Tankerness. Mansie had with him a dog which was much admired, the laird describing it as a perfect beauty. "No thanks to it," replied Mansie. "It's weel fed, weel housed, an' it's free o' debt, which is more than you or me can say, laird!" It seems that the laird had been due an account to Mansie, and this was the sly way that the old flesher took to remind him of the debt.

Mansie did a big smuggling business, but he was so clever in carrying the goods after they were landed that he could never be caught, though he had many narrow escapes. On one occasion the excise officers got a hint that a cargo of spirits had been landed in the East Mainland, and they were determined to keep a strict eye on Mansie's movements. They watched him going away with his cart one afternoon, and they patiently awaited his return. When the cart reached Kirkwall, however, it was empty. A hint of the danger had been conveyed to the old smuggler, and he coolly planted the gin in a ditch a short distance from the town, carrying it in after the excise officers had been deceived by the empty cart.

The gaugers at last began to suspect this trick, and resolved to go out the Holm Road and meet Mansie some miles from town. The night chosen was a very dark one and they concealed themselves behind a stone wall. At length they heard the rattle of a cart in the distance and were on the alert. As the vehicle got into line with them they pounced out upon poor Mansie, and there, sure enough, were some half dozen small kegs of gin and brandy. The officers were elated with their successful capture; but Mansie took the thing very coolly. He slipped the reins of his horse over its head and began to walk some distance in front, keeping the excisemen in roars of laughter as he recounted to them many of the best of his large stock of anecdotes. In this way time passed quickly, and when Mansie arrived opposite his own house at the head of the Clay Loan, he turned his horse inwards as if to unyoke. "No, no, Mansie," said the chief officer of excise, "you must bring your cart and its contents down to our premises. Seeing you have carried the spirits so far, you will not grudge taking them that extra distance." "Spirits," said Mansie in well-feigned surprise, "Whaur are they?" The officers went over to the cart to show the kegs to Mansie, but, alas, they were gone!

It is needless to say that the excisemen used some very strong language when they discovered that they had been outwitted by the sly old smuggler. Mansie to prevent accidents, was always accompanied by some friends when he went out on a smuggling expedition; and, knowing these were close at hand when he was caught by the excisemen, he depended upon them noiselessly removing the kegs from the cart whilst he kept the gaugers in good humour with his funny stories. The means that were taken to circumvent the excisemen were thus simple; but they were also effective.

On another occasion Mansie had brought a little keg of

spirits into town in broad daylight, and before he had time to get it hidden, he noticed an exciseman coming up the Clay Loan. Mansie, who was full of resource, lifted the keg and dropped it into the water barrel. When the exciseman arrived at the house the old smuggler was busy throwing water into the barrel.

"Well, Mansie," said the exciseman, "what is this that you are so busy about today?"

"Oh," replied Mansie, "my barrel was gizened, and I'm trying to get it put right wi' water from the well, as there's no appearance o' ony rain comin'."

Mansie kept so cool that the officer was completely taken in and passed on, though the old smuggler declared afterwards that he did fear that he was to be caught on that particular occasion.

Smuggling was carried on to such an extent, and with such bad effects upon the people that the Seceding clergymen began to denounce the traffic. One Sunday, Mansie's minister held forth on the iniquity of the trade and declared that no Christian would take any part in it. When the service was over, some person asked Mansie what he thought of the sermon.

"I think," answered Mansie, "that oor minister is no' very consistent, for at the very time he was preaching he had six kegs o' as guid brandy under his pulpit as ever was smuggled!"

This joke was much appreciated, for Mansie, being church officer, often hid his smuggled spirits under the floor of the pulpit, pretty confident that that would be one of the last places that the excisemen would think of searching.

Mansie was fond of practical joking, especially if indulging in it would assist him in his illicit trade. One night he wanted to bring in a quantity of spirits from Deerness, but was anxious to make sure that the excisemen should be out of the way. He met a man whom he suspected to be in league with the gaugers and told him in secret that he was to cross the Bridge of Wideford between twelve and one o'clock next morning with three horses laden with kegs. This news was conveyed to the excisemen, and they took up their position under the bridge so as to make a capture.

Just about one o'clock Mansie made his appearance, but he

was coming from, instead of to, the town, and the kegs which he carried were empty.

When asked for an explanation of his strange behaviour, Mansie said he had got the spirits into the town by another road, that he thought it would be a pity to keep the excisemen out all night in the cold, and that he had therefore come out to tell them that their watch was in vain!

On another occasion the excisemen got a hint that Mansie was to convey a number of kegs from Holm, that he was to carry them in "caisies" slung over the backs of horses, and that he was to avoid the public road and cross the heather. The officers accordingly made up their minds they would circumvent the old smuggler, and spread themselves over the moor in such a way that it was impossible he could escape if he came that way.

Mansie, however, had his scouts, and these gave him "wittance" of the nice little scheme that had been laid to capture him. He therefore piloted his kegs into town by the public road, in the mirk of night, leaving the gaugers to their cold and lonely bed among the heather. With "the skreigh o' day" the officers came to Mansie's house, but by that time the "grice" and been safely planted. The old smuggler was therefore in a kindly mood and laid before the officers some of the Holland, which he had just smuggled, to cheer them after their cold night's vigil. "Grand gin," said one of the officers, "where did you get it?" His host did not enlighten him on this point, but very pertinently reminded him of the text that runs: "Eat such things as are set before you, asking no question!"

In the winter of 1827-28, a vessel was brought into Kirkwall harbour with a cargo of oats which had been somewhat damaged. Those in authority decided to throw the grain overboard because it was not worth the duty payable upon it. When they began operations, Mansie appeared on the scene. Having equipped himself with some fishing tackle, he went with his boat and cast his anchor a little to windward of where the grain was being thrown into the sea, and paid out the boat's line until he came alongside of the vessel. Those in authority saw that Mansie was getting his boat filled with the oats, and ordered him away. "I cam' oot tae fish, an' ye'll sink me boat if ye keep haevin' thae aits in her this waye," was Mansie's cool reply. When his boat was well filled he went to the shore and secured his "fang." Others contented themselves with gathering up the oats after they had been washed ashore. After the grain had been secured it was washed with fresh water and dried on kilns, some of it being made into meal and some sown as seed and cropped. For this kind of smuggling they were not fined.

Once Mansie was very hard pressed at Holm. He was carrying a keg on his shoulders when some rangers saw him and gave pursuit. Striking off the road he made straight for a farmhouse with the excisemen close in pursuit. After a race of about half a mile, Mansie was captured, but the keg he was carrying was empty! The people at the farm, who had witnessed the chase, secured an empty keg, and when Mansie was passing through the close which separated the house from the byre they exchanged casks with him. Fortunately the excisemen took the view that Mansie had hoaxed them and made no search of the farmhouse where the gin had been dropped.

At length Mansie was taken before the Session for smuggling, and he lost his situation as beadle. He took this so much to heart that he gave up attending church. One day the minister met Mansie and said: "Mansie, you never come to church now." O, what a lee," retorted Mansie. "My wife is there every Sunday." "But that is not you," urged the minister. "Well," replied Mansie, "when I was maerit, the minister telt me wife an' me that we wis ane, an' if we are no' ane, either you or the other minister has telt us a lee!"

A STENNESS STILL

Before the new road was made between Kirkwall and Stromness, there was little traffic in the vicinity of the Standing Stones of Stenness. An inn stood near the Bridge of Waithe, however, which was sometimes visited by tramps and packmen in those days. One night a Highland packman was staying at this hostelry, and before retiring to rest he went for a stroll round the margin of the loch. As he was crossing the promontory under the farm of Deepdale it struck him that the place had a hollow sound. Upon going down on his knees and removing one or two loose turfs, he was not a little astonished at finding a small still. When he returned to his lodgings he mentioned his discovery, but from the handsome way he was treated, and the anxiety of his inmates to get him to keep the matter a secret, he suspected that they knew who the proprietor was. He watched the place, and very soon he saw a neighbouring farmer working the still. Shortly after this he observed the farmer going into Stromness with a cart, and he seated himself in the vehicle. During his ride the pedlar found that the cart was well filled with straw, and that each "winlin" had in the heart of it a keg of whisky. Upon arriving at Stromness the packman left the cart, but kept his eye on the farmer. Ultimately the straw was carried into a well-known public-house there, and the pedlar was thus convinced that he knew the smuggler's chief customer. Some time afterwards this same farmer was driving along the road homewards from the Birsay direction. The night was clear and frosty, and everything was so quiet that the lonely traveller thought he had the road to himself. All at once, however, a couple of gaugers pounced upon him, and demanded to see the contents of the sacks which were lying in his cart. Resistance was useless, and the sacks were at once examined. They contained altogether something like a dozen bushels of malt, and the experienced eyes of the gaugers were not slow in discovering that the grain had been prepared not for ale, but for whisky. The farmer was accompanied home by the officers when a thorough search was made for the still. The smuggler pled ignorance of such apparatus, but the officers prosecuted the search, and it was noticed that they went straight to the promontory below the farm of Deepdale. They removed the covering there, but the still was gone, and it was never found. It did duty for many years afterwards, but in a different spot. As to the pedlar, the people strongly suspected him of acting the traitor, and he would have got a warm reception if he had ever again been caught in Stenness.

SMUGGLING IN THE WEST MAINLAND

A good deal of smuggling was at one time done at the farm of Tormiston in Stenness. The tenant there took out a licence for making a little malt for his own use, and the excisemen came at intervals to measure the grain so as to make sure that the revenue was not cheated. Quite close to the farm there was a trout-house, so overgrown with bushes that its presence was never suspected by strangers. The tenant of the farm usually kept a good supply of malt hidden there, and he carried on his smuggling operations so carefully that when the officer came to take measurements he had always the quantity in his possession. He managed to defraud the Excise in this way for many years, but at last a neighbour informed on him and he was heavily fined.

Some people in Birsay at one time rigged up a still in an old disused quarry in the hill in that parish. Whisky was said to have been manufactured in large quantities there for a long period; but when the law became more stringent, and the owners of the land on which stills were found were liable to prosecution, the smugglers gave up the trade. At the time the still referred to was erected, the quarry was common property; but after the hill was divided, the proprietor of the quarry, thinking the risk too great, ordered the apparatus to be removed.

Another still was successfully carried on for a long time in Sandwick, in one of the caves along the coast. The place was secluded, and there was a plentiful supply of water; but the smoke necessary for carrying on operations attracted so much attention that the smugglers ultimately stopped the work on their own accord.

On one occasion, a nice little still reached Kirkwall as a hamper of apples. It was subsequently dispatched to the West Mainland, were it was successfully wrought for many years; but after the owner died, the risk connected with the business was so great that no one was found bold enough to renew operations with it.

HOW A PUBLICAN OVER-REACHED HIMSELF

Some years ago there lived in the vicinity of Kirkwall a pious farmer, much esteemed by his neighbours, but who thought, with many others, that it was no sin to make his own barley into malt and sell his "mountain dew" to the best advantage, notwithstanding the Excise regulations. The publican in town with whom he usually dealt, for some selfish reason, informed the Excise officer that this farmer was coming in on a certain night with some smuggled whisky. The officer accordingly met him just as he was entering the town. The farmer, seeing what was up, took off his cap and, reverently looking up, said, "Oh, Lord, hast thou betrayed me?" "No, it's not He, but your precious merchant that did it," replied the officer; "however, get you to your destination, deliver your goods, and leave for home again without delay." The farmer thanked him, and did as instructed. A few minutes after he had left the town, the officer apprehended the publican and seized the whisky.

A COPINSAY SMUGGLER

James Dennison, Copinsay, was a noted smuggler in his day and had some curious adventures. Once, when acting as a pilot, he was carried to America. After he retired from farming, he resided at Kirkwall, and conferred a great benefit on the town by opening up the Walliwall Quarry. His was the first house built of stones taken from that place. When in Copinsay he had a vault in the kiln barn, which he used for keeping his whisky after it was bottled, but his still was situated in the almost inaccessible cliffs at Melders. It having reached the ears of the excisemen that James manufactured both ale and whisky, an officer was dispatched to Copinsay. When that gentleman landed, Andrew Dennison shouldered a "cubby" and ran to the Lee, the gauger following him till he went down on the "Doggie Benckie." After a time young Dennison returned and invited the gauger to pay a visit to the distillery. Needless to say, he declined to take the journey along a narrow, sloping, slippery ledge in the face of a perpendicular cliff 200 feet above the sea. Andrew, knowing that the people at home had meantime been busy hiding all the contraband articles in the house, and his ruse having been more successful than he had dared to hope, became very affable and asked the gauger into the house, where he was entertained with even more than the customary hospitality extended by his parents to all who visited the lonely isle. Dennison sent his whisky to the town. His plan of operations was to bottle the spirits, and start with a lot of farm produce in his boat, the bottles being concealed beneath. When he approached the town he put the bottles ashore, hiding them among the seaweed, and then proceeded to the pier with his boat in the evening. When his customers learned of his arrival they soon contrived to assist him in the work of bringing in the bottles.

A COMMON TRICK

Thomas Dick, a young man over six feet in height, one day noticing a gauger approaching his father's house, determined to try and save the malt by a common trick. He lifted a sack of chaff on his shoulders and ran down over the brae, taking care that the gauger should see him hurrying away. The officer spurred up his horse, and Tom took refuge in a quagmire. The gauger followed, but his horse soon stuck in the mud. Young Dick then threw down the sack and offered to help the gauger to take his horse out on to firm ground; but before this was done his father had got the malt safely out of reach of the excise. The gauger, when he discovered how he had been tricked, lost his temper. Telling the tale afterwards, old James Dick would say, "Bewoath man, the gauger was a mein pugso o' a fellow, and I thought 'at Tammie an' him wad been in a girdifuff on thae flair, for Tammie widna let him turn everything upside doon." However, no blows were really struck.

"PEEDIE BANNETS"

A nother noted smuggler, James Smith, was known as "Peedie Bannets." He resided in Stenness, and carried on smuggling in Stromness. When driving his grey mare on the road, if he happened to meet a gauger he never failed to present his snuff-box, and then began to tell some funny anecdotes of which he seemed to have an unlimited store. In this way he succeeded in interesting the gauger until his mare had passed on with the contraband. One morning, however, a sly gauger made a capture. "Peedie Bannets," who was a man of resource, took down the reins, adjusted the bridle, and began to walk before the mare in the fashion common to his class then. Whilst doing so, he was so lively and jocose that he kept the gauger (elated as he was by the seizure he had made) laughing so loudly that he never missed the sound of the mare's feet, and when he looked around at the head of Hamliboe the animal had disappeared as well as the lead.

The lead consisted of two caisies, each known as half a lead, and were hung on either side of the clibber which was on the mare's back. The clibber was made of four pieces of wood, and was somewhat like a cart saddle. The lead and the clibber, however, have now given way to the cart, just as the latter has been followed by the motor.

The following may be taken as a specimen of "Peedie Bannets' " conversational powers. Seated in a public house with a cronie, a stoup or can in one hand and the other resting on his knee in the inside of the enormous piece of headgear from which he derived his name, he would say, "Deed, gossip, I pat Johnnie tae th' toon ae time an' I gaed him a pound, an' th' witless blockhead bought a grand hat mead oot o' dog hair, an' me auld breeks, sistdu, an' paid eighteen shillings for hid; an' he only haed hid on twa or three times till hid was uiseless. If he haed only bought a bannet like me ane, hid wid only cost him tree shillings an' wad laisted him for years." This wonderful bonnet was very large and of the kind worn by staid merchants in those days. It was so big that "Peedie Bannets" could lay the edge on his shoulder, as he always did, and pull it down to windward.

A LENIENT GAUGER

The gaugers were not tyrants always. One of them, called William McKing, was a kindly sort of man, and Gibbie Cormack, the innkeeper, called his youngest son after him. When he was baptised an old woman got the name so mixed in her head that she thought he had been baptised in the king's name, and went home and said, "Sic a waye tae bapteeze a bairn, ca'in' him Willie in the King's neem." Once a boat came from Stroma with whisky, and Gibbie got a cask of it. Mr McKing saw it and had to make a seizure, but he hinted to the owner to keep most of the whisky. The hoops were eventually knocked off the cask, and the owner declared it had been driven ashore, and his statement was accepted.

A LIVELY TALE

John Esson was born in Deerness shortly after the news of Bonaparte's defeat at Waterloo reached that parish. As a genial and obliging man he had few peers; and as a merchant he was for a long time successful. At length, however, he met with a great misfortune. He went to an adjoining island to pay some fishermen, and on the journey he lost all his money. This caused him to reduce his operations. As a daring smuggler he had an adventure such as few experienced. When he was in a London company's employment he had to go to Longhope for eggs and to sell goods. While there he bought a cask of rum, and, getting a fresh breeze, he sailed out of Longhope. No sooner had he reached the open water, however, than he saw the cutter's boat following him. Knowing that a chase in smooth water would end in his capture, he said, "No fear, boys; we'll do them yet. Every man to his post and we'll try her across the Firth. They canna pull in the choppy sea, and the tide will tak' us to windward like a steamer, so that we will be able to run into Hoy Mouth with the next tide." When the smuggler's boat entered the fall of the tide a cowardly lump of sea struck the boat on the quarter, broached her to, and half filled her. In an instant the peak was dropped and the bowline brought to windward. After the boat was again brought into working trim, the mainsail was reefed, the small jib set, and the cask was once more made secure. The smuggler now looked for his pursuers, but they had found the hunt too risky and had turned back. The water was then pumped out of the boat, and when the tide turned a position was reached from which it was comparatively easy to sail into Hoy Sound. After this adventure Esson was more cautious and did not try to smuggle when there was any chance of his being captured. Subsequently, however, he innocently suffered a very heavy penalty from a band of French smugglers. A French vessel having landed some contraband goods and hidden them from the coastguard, some persons found them and appropriated them to their own use. The Frenchmen retaliated by poisoning the cattle nearest to the place. The beasts happened to belong to Mr Esson.

A HUMOROUS SMUGGLER

John Delday was another smuggler in Deerness. He lived in Ouse, and was caretaker of Mr Groat's cottage at Mirkady. It was supposed that he acted for a merchant in Kirkwall. His plan was to go aboard vessels when they came into Deersound to wait for a fair wind, and receive a supply of spirits. When he got the cargo into Newhall Cottage he made it up into handy sizes and locked it in suitable presses. Of these presses he was not supposed to have the keys. Then he generally got his next neighbour, Edward Omond, to accompany him to the town in his boat. The boat having been moored alongside the West Pier at Kirkwall, they left her and others removed the goods. The cargo having thus been disposed of, they would quietly slip down to the boat, unmoor her and return home. When the first temperance lecturer, a well-known Edinburgh divine, addressed a meeting of fishermen in the parish, John took a bottle and glass and offered him a dram. This, of course was declined, and John said, "Here's luck to you, sir; but if, you had been as often at the back of Auskerry on a bad night, in an open boat, as A'm been, ye wad like a dram as weel as me!" During the burst of laughter which followed this speech, the contents of the glass disappeared. After the commotion had abated, the lecturer said, "Now, my honest fellow, I hope you'll tell me what religion you are of?" John replied, "The horse's creed." "What are the chief points in that creed?" was the stranger's next question. "Tae wirk weel a' the week, an' gang tae the grass on Sunday," was John's unexpected reply. The audience roared, and the lecturer could barely keep his gravity; but he soon calmed his hearers and told them that he believed many of them liked a dram as well as the party who had so boldly shown his colours. This incident furnished the lecturer with a special theme for his future addresses.

PART II—PRESS-GANG STORIES

PRESS-GANG STORIES

Every parish in the county has got its press-gang stories, but the generation which took a part in making the history of that time has passed away. Half a century ago volumes of anecdotes on the subject might easily have been written; but those thrilling tales can only be picked up now with difficulty from descendants of the men who took part in, or were witnesses of, the stirring events which occurred when George III was King.

The practice of impressing seamen to man the Royal Navy commenced in England as early as 1355, immediately after the country had been desolated by a noisome pestilence, which had scarcely left a single State of Europe or Asia free from its ravages, and which had swept away almost a third of the inhabitants wherever it came. It is computed that about fifty thousand perished in London alone.

The first authentic information we have been able to glean regarding the press-gang in Orkney, however, is in *Glimpses of Kirkwall and its People in the Olden Time*. In that work, a minute of Town Council, dated March 17, 1692, is quoted, in which it is stated that the King had resolved that no seamen of his kingdom be pressed for the future. But His Majesty went on to command that the Town Council should make up an exact list of the seamen and fishermen who had refused to join the service, so that the men wanted shall be drawn by lot. It was at the close of the eighteenth and the beginning of the nineteenth centuries, however, that the press-gang became particularly oppressive, and we know, from the work already quoted, that Kirkwall Town Council, during that period, was often called upon to provide men for His Majesty's service.

What made the press-gang so active during the period dealt with in the following stories was the outbreak of the Revolutionary War in 1792. "France," as one historian has put it, "considered itself entitled to advance the Revolution and the rights of man wherever its own arms or popular insurrection gave it command. Britain denied the right of any power to annul the political system of Europe at its pleasure. No more serious, no more sufficient ground of war ever existed between two nations; still, the event proved that, with the highest justification for war, the highest wisdom would yet have chosen peace. Britain's entry into the war converted it from an affair of two or three campaigns into a struggle of twenty years, ending in more violent convulsions, more widespread misery, and more atrocious crimes, than in all probability would have resulted in the temporary triumph of the Revolutionary cause in 1793."

Under their renowned leader, Napoleon, the enthusiastic French soldiery were marching from one end of Europe to the other in their professed attempt to give "liberty" to the people. Some of the powers, however, notably Britain, objected to be set at "liberty" by the French method. They preferred the freedom they already enjoyed, and were not at all enamoured of the Gallic way of reaching " the perfectability of the species." Hence the wars with France.

Never did greater glory attend the British arms than at that time. In the southern corner of Europe, Wellington, with a handful of British soldiers, was keeping the myriad warriors of "the scourger of the world" at bay.

The British leader, unlike Napoleon, was very careful of the lives of his soldiers, yet from time to time the shattered ranks had to be recruited—men had to be found to fill up the gaps which were being made both in the army and navy. This gave rise to the press-gang. As a sufficient number of men could not be found to enlist of their own free will, each district in the country had again and again to supply a certain quota of soldiers and sailors; and for every man that was not forthcoming, a sum of £40 had to be paid.

Young, able-bodied men were thus always in danger of being impressed, and various methods were adopted by them to elude the press-gang. Holes were made under the floors of the houses for the purpose of giving a handy hiding-place, and recesses were cunningly formed in peat-stacks for a similar purpose. Those who were afraid to risk such places of concealment went off to the crags, or roamed from morning till night amongst the hills. In harvest time, when people were sharing, horses were usually kept within easy distance, to provide a means of escape; and the mothers and daughters were often placed on some eminence to watch for and signal the approach of the dreaded press-gang. Occasionally the fair sex assumed an aggressive attitude, and in one case in Sandwick, a woman, in protecting a young man, attacked a constable with a shearing hook. It is said the weapon entered the constable's side and that the wound proved fatal.

In press-gang times many young men from Orkney went to the whale fishing at Davis Straits, and were often impressed on their return home. Three or four natives of Sandwick who had been captured in this way were, in the course of war, taken by the enemy, and were kept about seven years in a French prison. One of these, a shoemaker by trade, occupied his time in captivity in making shoes for the soldiers. He is said to have been such an adept at the work that he put as many as two pairs through his hands each day, and was thus able to save a little money to bring home with him after peace was proclaimed.

The mode of choosing the men who were to be dispatched to the seat of war was very simple. A few of the landlords and principal tenants in a parish met in private and selected any of their neighbours whom they thought fit. A list of the names was handed to the press-gang or constables, many of whom were natives, as strangers would not have known the people or their residences. The men whom it was agreed to impress were not known to the general inhabitants. All were therefore in dread of being captured, and kept out of the way. On the other hand, if the constables met a person likely to be suitable for the service, they were not very particular whether he had been specially named to them or not, and took him prisoner.

Sufficient will be found in the following press-gang stories to illustrate the remark of Thackeray, that in this war every blow struck by a soldier on the field of battle wounded horribly some other innocent heart perhaps thousands of miles away; and that the war levied its contributions equally on the women with the men, taking the tears of the former and the blood of the latter. Perhaps it never entered the mind of Napoleon once to think that his ambition was yielding fruit in sorrow-laden and broken hearts even in these far-off isles of the northern main. And yet it was so, for many fathers, sons, or brothers who were ruthlessly torn from their homes by the press-gang never returned. They either died on the field of battle or found a last resting-place in the depths of the ocean.

A STIFF TUSSLE AT FINGEROW

Often in the harvest season, in those stirring times, the people of Orkney had great difficulty in getting their crops in. All the cutting at that time had to be done with the hook, and whilst the men were engaged at the work a sharp watch had to be kept in all directions, for the dreaded press-gang might heave in sight at any moment.

One morning, the people on the little croft of Fingerow, Scapa, near Kirkwall, thought they might risk to commence cutting. The press-gang had not been seen in the district for some days, and it was hoped they had given up the search there as fruitless.

Thomas Sinclair, who was in charge of Fingerow, therefore went down with his hook to a field of bere below the house, but he had only got a small patch of the crop cut when he received a signal that the press-gang were approaching. He had no time to escape down the face of the cliffs, which had been his usual hiding-place, so he crept away into the middle of the field of bere.

The two officers who were in search of him—Peter Wick and Joseph Tait—poked into every corner and cranny of the house and were closely followed by Sinclair's sister, who had, our informant states, a dreadful tongue. As Wick and Tait

visited one place after another on the croft without finding their man, Kirsty Sinclair, who was armed with a shearing hook, gave a derisive cheer, at the same time waving over her head the rusty weapon she carried.

The conduct of Kirsty, however, instead of driving the officers off the place as was intended, only made them the more determined in their search, as they were sure that Sinclair was somewhere on the croft. When they reached the field of bere and saw one small patch cut they concluded that their man was probably hidden amongst the long straw.

That the search might be thorough, Wick went down one rig whilst Tait went up the other. The officers were thus slowly but surely drawing closer upon Sinclair and made a rush for him. Sinclair, a coarse, heavy fellow, determined to fight for his liberty and struck out at Tait with a heavy batten of wood. The attack was so sudden that with one blow he laid the officer senseless. Peter Wick, the other constable, then rushed upon Sinclair, and the two had a severe encounter. Wick, however, was an old "Nor'-Waster," with a powerful arm, and he struck out so effectually with his fists that his opponent was speedily put *hors de combat.*

Kirsty Sinclair meantime was not idle. Thinking the press-gang had killed her brother, she rushed up behind Wick with the hook she had in her hand and dealt a terrible blow at the back of his head. Fortunately for the officer the point of the weapon stuck in the collar of his coat, and before the enraged woman could get it out to use it again, she was thrown to the ground beside her brother.

It turned out that Tait had merely been stunned by the blow he had received, and in a short time he was able to return to Kirkwall, with the assistance of his companion. As for the Sinclairs—brother and sister— they were left lying in the field bleeding and helpless.

Some war vessels happened to be anchored in Kirkwall Bay at the time, and the town officers having reported that they had been badly used at Fingerow, a few sailors were sent ashore to assist in bringing Sinclair into town.

That same night Wick returned to Fingerow, accompanied by the man-of-war's men, dragged Sinclair out of bed and told him he was their prisoner. The poor man was ill-fitted for such a journey after the mauling which he had received earlier in the day, and he frequently lay down on the road. Some of the sailors, however, had a "ratten" which they vigorously applied to Sinclair's back on such occasions, so that before he reached the town his skin was all broken.

When he was taken before a doctor next day, the poor fellow's body was such a mass of sores that he was considered unfit for service in the navy, and he was therefore sent home again. As he had, however, resisted the town's officers in the discharge of their duties, and had attacked them with a bludgeon, his only cow was taken from him and presented to Tait as damages for the injuries he had received.

Kirsty Sinclair had a sad end. Some years subsequently, she went into her sister-in-law's house, asked her to go out on a trifling message, and in her absence hammered a large pin into the head of a little child that was lying in a cradle. For this crime she was taken to Edinburgh, where she was tried and hanged—being the last Orcadian who was executed for murder.

A Mother's Watchfulness

George Firth, a young man belonging to Finstown, narrowly escaped being captured. He had been away at Davis Straits, and his vessel ran into Stromness to discharge the Orkney portion of the crew. The press-gang were on the alert to get some of these men when on their way home from Stromness. George Firth's mother came to know of this, and made up her mind to save her son. Accordingly, she tramped all the way from Finstown to Stromness with a bundle of women's clothes on her back, and when she met her son there, she dressed him up like an old woman, wrapping up his head in shawls, as if he were suffering from a bad attack of toothache. When about a couple of miles from Stromness, mother and son met the press-gang, but the disguise was so complete that the pair were allowed to pass unmolested. During the few months that Firth subsequently stayed at home he was hunted night and day, so that much of his time was spent out on the hills, and even in pig- and other outhouses. Such a sharp lookout did his mother keep on the movements of the press-gang, however, they were never able to capture him. On his next voyage to Davis Straits his vessel got nipped in the ice, and he, having rendered some valuable assistance in getting her off, when he reached London, received a reward of £100.

MARRIED IN SPITE OF THE PRESS-GANG

Men who had been out in the North-West were in great demand for the navy, and were often picked off their vessels when in sight of their island homes.

At the period we refer to, Orkney and Shetland largely supplied the crews of the whalers, and when the men returned from a successful fishing in the Arctic regions, the opportunity was considered a favourable one for entering into the matrimonial state.

Robert Miller, a Kirkwall man, had returned from the Davis Straits one autumn with the intention of getting married, but when he landed in Orkney he found that the press-gang were busy at work, and he had to go into hiding.

His friends so built their peat stack that he was able to crawl into the centre of it whenever he got the hint that the officers of the press-gang were in the vicinity.

He had made up his mind, however, that he would be married, and all preparations were made for the great event with as much secrecy as possible.

The company had gathered and the minister was in the house of the bride, prepared to proceed with the ceremony, when the dreaded press-gang made its appearance. The ladies are not usually of a bellicose disposition, but when they saw in this instance a likelihood of the marriage being spoiled by these interlopers, they rose up in wrath against them and assailed the members of the press-gang both with tongue and missiles, so that these gentlemen were glad to beat a very hasty retreat.

After this little episode, a back window of the house was lifted and the bridegroom, dressed in woman's clothes, bounded into the room.

The doors having been barricaded to prevent a surprise, the clergyman proceeded to perform the ceremony, and surely no bridegroom was ever married in such strange garb.

Later in the evening the press-gang returned, when Miller was engaged dancing a reel, but whether they were unable to recognise him, or whether they were once more driven off the premises by the ladies, we have been unable to learn. One thing is certain, however, and that is, that they did not get their man. He was spared for many years afterwards, and was the first beadle of the Kirkwall Free Church.

A NASTY TRICK

The name of Robert Mowat, a weaver's constable, was held in evil repute by the people in Kirkwall. He had an apprentice, whose name we have been unable to ascertain, whom he used in a very scurvy manner. The lad had faithfully served his apprenticeship with Mowat, and the day his time was out, his master, who acted as one of the press-gang, apprehended him. Very probably this young man never returned to his native town, seeing that his name has been forgotten, but the shabby trick of his master was talked of for years afterwards.

HUNTED LIKE A WILD BEAST

Robert Yorston was a contemporary of Robert Miller, who got married under such trying circumstances; and, if we mistake not, his wife was "best maid" at that wedding. Robert was a shoemaker to trade, but to support his widowed mother he had to go to the Davis Straits fishing. On one occasion when he returned he was hunted like a wild beast from island to island by the press-gang. For twelve weeks he was concealed by a Mr Scott, in Victoria Street, Kirkwall, but after that he was all over the Mainland and in the North and South Isles, ever ruthlessly followed by the press-gang.

Robert Yorston's grandfather had entered the navy

voluntarily, but he did not like it. He caught a severe cold when in the service, and returned to Kirkwall, where he died at the early age of 46.

His uncle, David Gorie (a brother of Dr. Gorie), was pressed for the navy. Being well educated he rose to be sailing-master; but he was of the opinion that little money could be made in the service of His Majesty George III, so he left it, bought a ship of his own, sailed for South America and was never heard of again in Orkney.

Robert Yorston always expressed himself as adverse to entering the navy. He neither wished to kill people, he said, nor did he have a desire to be killed himself, and he therefore took every precaution to avoid the attentions of the press-gang. And though he had many hair-breadth escapes he was never captured.

He lived till he was over a century old, and the inhabitants of Kirkwall showed their respect for him on his attaining the age of one hundred years by presenting him with a purse of sovereigns.

TRICKING THE PRESS-GANG

A very good story is told of how one man escaped serving his King and country. He was being hotly pursued by the press-gang through Kirkwall, when he took refuge in a garden in Victoria Street. At that time each of the houses on the west side of the street had a jetty running into the Peerie Sea, which was used for taking in peats, and occasionally for landing supplies of smuggled goods.

The man we have been referring to (his name seems to be forgotten now), got the hint that his pursuers had a suspicion of his hiding-place, so he plunged into the Peerie Sea and made his way up past where Grainbank House now stands.

Away in the distance he could see the press-gang hurrying along the route he had so recently trod himself and he was convinced that his capture would only be a matter of a few minutes.

Necessity, however, is the mother of invention. He resolved

to secure his freedom by strategy. He therefore stripped off all his clothing, rolled himself in a bed of nettles, and then dressed himself before the press-gang came on the scene.

His captors indulged in some chaff at the expense of their prisoner, because he had allowed himself to be so easily caught. The answer he gave was that if they had been as ill as he was, perhaps they would have shown quite as little inclination to indulge in running.

In the natural course of events the man was taken before a doctor, and when he was examined his body was found to be one mass of blisters. The doctor, believing the captive was suffering from some sort of skin disease, refused to pass him. The man did not grudge the price he had paid for his freedom.

A CRUEL BAIT

But the press-gang were just as good at trickery as were the people, and sometimes they adopted most abominable tactics for getting recruits for the service.

Early last century there was a public house in Bridge Street, Kirkwall, which was kept by a man named Scollay. This was a favourite resort for the press-gang, especially on market days, and not a few young men got into trouble there. The method adopted for pressing unsuspecting people was somewhat as follows. One of the press-gang would take up a position at a window upstairs, whilst two of his companions were secreted near the front of the building on the ground floor. If a likely-looking young man was seen passing along the street, the officer of the press-gang dropped a shilling over the window. Naturally enough, the youth stopped, picked it up, and whilst he was wondering who the owner might be, the press-gang pounced upon him.

The King's baton was laid on the dupe's shoulders, and he was blandly told that, seeing he had accepted the shilling he would now have to go and serve His Majesty the King by land or sea.

Many a young man was captured in this way, and there can be no question that such tactics as these helped considerably to arouse the feelings of the working classes against the press-gang.

A Narrow Escape

William Heddle, a labouring man in Shapinsay, on one occasion had a narrow escape from being captured by the press-gang. It seems that when men were wanted in Shapinsay, a meeting of the principal farmers in the island was generally held in the Parish Church, that a selection might be made.

At one of these gatherings the tenant of Weyland (the house is now known as Strathore), recommended that William Heddle should be impressed. The tenant of Weyland had asked Heddle to work to him shortly before as a harvest hand, but the latter had declined on the ground that he had no shoes. The fact was that at that time tanning leather at home was an illicit trade, but notwithstanding this, the tenant of Weyland had prepared a horse hide for his own use, and had refused to give Heddle a bit of it as a part of his harvest fee. This led to bad feeling between the parties—hence the proposal that Heddle should be impressed.

Heddle, however, got the hint, and he took care for a long time afterwards to give his own house a wide berth. Night after night he roamed the hills, seeking shelter in caves or in dry ditches. On one occasion he was stealthily approaching his own house for the purpose of getting a night's rest, when he heard footsteps in the distance.

The nearest hiding-place was the graveyard. He therefore clambered over the wall and hid among the tombstones. As he lay there the press-gang passed, and he heard plans being discussed for his capture. After visiting his house his pursuers made a thorough search in the vicinity, but were either too superstitious to enter the graveyard or thought it a very unlikely place for Heddle to hide in, for they did not go near it.

Heddle was never taken. From the time that he heard the press-gang arranging how to capture him he carried an old gun and a knife, and he always declared that he would defend himself to the death with these. It is quite likely that the press-gang knew of this resolve, and also that he was a man who would stick to his word, for they did not show any great desire to put his threat to the test. The tenant of Weyland also suffered for the part he played in the transaction. So long as Heddle carried the gun and knife he was in terror for his life, and he never knew what rest was till he was assured that these weapons had been laid aside.

A HARSH PROCEEDING

One very effecting scene was witnessed in press-gang times in Birsay. Widow Hourston, Hozen, had been left with a young child to face the battle of life. Through all her struggles she was cheered by the thought that her son John, when he reached manhood, would be able to work the farm for her. But these bright dreams were never realised. One morning the hated press-gang made its appearance at Hozen and demanded her only son—he whom she had relied upon to be the support and comfort of her old age.

She pled, as only a mother can plead in such circumstances, that her son might be left to her. But no heed was given to her entreaties. "Tak' my only coo, but leave my son," was her final appeal. Even this had no weight, and John Hourston therefore resolved that he should make one bold attempt to secure his freedom by "rinnin' doon a flag" on the other side of the house or byre. The effort proved abortive, however, for one of the constables who went round there saw him forcing his way through a hole in the roof, rushed up to the place, seized the unfortunate man by the hair of the head, and so secured him.

Hourston was eventually carried away to fight the French, and though he himself survived the war, his mother did not, for she died of a broken heart.

Of all the iniquitous actions of the press-gang in Birsay, none aroused a more general feeling of execration than the capture of John Hourston. The old lady who supplied the above information was born in "the year o' the peace," which was also the year of blood—"the crowning carnage, Waterloo."

As she told the story a suspicious moisture could be detected in the eyes of the good old woman, and it might truly be said of her that "the greet was i' her craig."

Though Hourston returned to England, he never visited Orkney, giving as his reason that he was afraid if he met any of his captors, who were then alive, he might be tempted to punish them for what they had done to him and his. Perhaps the fact that his mother had died in his absence, and that the young lady he had been courting had, whilst he was fighting his country's battles, married another, may also have influenced him in his resolve not to return to his native place.

A Token and a Sign

In press-gang times a number of young people were enjoying their Yule or New Year's Feast at the farm house of the "Umest Place"—the farm hard by the old palace in the Barony of Birsay. Fun and frolic were running high, when all at once the dread cry ran through the building that the press-gang were approaching. Amongst those present was the "hairst man," John Johnston, locally known in his day as Johnnie o' Smerchants, and Sandy Cumloquoy. There was a strong suspicion that these were the parties wanted for the King's service, and they naturally made up their minds to make a rush for their freedom.

Finding it impossible to get horses, the two set off on foot. According to our informant, Cumloquoy "could rin—thu sees some canna rin like ithers"—and he thus escaped at that time. His companion, however, was less successful, for he was captured somewhere amongst the houses in the direction of the north side of the parish.

As Johnnie o' Smerchants was being brought back past the old palace, he was met by his sweetheart, Kitty Cumloquoy. Kitty was almost distracted when she saw her lover being led away a prisoner by the press-gang. She "murmelted" sorely the hard fate which so rudely parted her from her Johnnie, especially at such a festive season; but she determined that he should not leave his native place without a farewell gift.

Accordingly she parcelled up some Christmas cheer in the shape of bread and cheese, and just as the press-gang were tearing her lover from her arms, she placed her love offering in his hands.

It so happened that Johnnie o' Smerchants, in the course of his service, was drafted into the same vessel with one of his captors, a sergeant who had been foremost in "gripping" him. This man had committed some offence, as a punishment for which he was sentenced to receive a number of lashes. Johnnie, curiously enough, was one of the sailors who was told off to administer the "cat," and he applied it with such a pith to the hurdies of his old enemy that the commander of the squad, at the finish of the punishment, exclaimed, "That man did his duty."

When Johnnie o' Smerchants got his discharge and returned to his island home, Kitty Cumloquoy was still single. He called on her, and showed her the bread and cheese she had given him on that doleful day when they were wrenched from each other's arms. Through all the battles in which he had been engaged he had carried it as a token and for a sign.

Under such circumstances it is almost needless to add that Kitty very willingly bestowed her heart and hand, and the marriage of the happy couple was celebrated shortly after the lover's return, with great rejoicing.

AN EASY CAPTURE

George Sinclair, a servant at Eastabist, Birsay, was captured with very little ceremony. The factor had been unable to secure a man for the parish, and he at last resolved that George should be the victim. All the factor's movements were closely watched, however, so that he had to adopt a little strategy to make the capture. He let it be known amongst his neighbours that on a certain day he was going to the Hillside "whassico," or ostensibly, to see a bit of land that was being enclosed at Farafield; but at the same time he laid his plans privately to get hold of Geordie. Instead of going to Farafield, he therefore quietly dropped into Eastabist, where he found poor Geordie taking his dinner. The young man had been off taking some "floss," and when the press-gang entered the house he was bare-footed. He slipped "ben" and tried to hide in an out-of-the-way corner there, but it was no use. Some of the constables seized him, the factor laid the official staff on his shoulder, and he became "a King's man," and was marched off to fight his country's battle, whether he liked it or not.

This young lad's half-brother, George Stockan, had a curious experience. He happened to be along with others at the house of Nether Skelday, Birsay, on a Hallowe'en Eve, practising some of the spells which were in vogue at that particular season in the olden time. One of these was to climb up the bere stack "backlins," and whatever they saw beneath them in the darkness was held to be symbolic of their future fate. Stockan tried his fortune in this way, and declared that he saw, spread out underneath him, the blue sea. He subsequently went to sea, lived a sailor's life, and was ultimately drowned.

A SUBSTITUTE

At another time a man was badly needed for Birsay, but nobody would volunteer, and those who were fit and able went into hiding. The people were in a great state of excitement, for they did not know the moment when a father, son, or brother might be lifted by the press-gang. It so happened, however, that a vessel had been wrecked off the coast and the whole crew had been lost, with the exception of one man, the carpenter of the ship. The natives had shown great kindness to this unfortunate sailor, and he in gratitude offered to serve on behalf of the parish—an offer which was gladly accepted.

A STRANGE MEETING

On one occasion, when the Birsay fishing boats were out at sea, a war vessel hove in sight, made up to them, and seized some of the fishermen. The captain ordered the prisoners aboard his ship and demanded their names. When Robert Cumloquoy announced his name, the captain took him down to his cabin, where the two were closeted for a long time. After this interview, the captain came on deck and asked the prisoners to point out the houses to him were he was likely to find young men suitable for sailors. The reply which he received was that all men available for the service would have taken to the hills immediately they noticed his vessel in the offing. Upon hearing this, the captain set the fishermen free and immediately afterwards put his vessel to sea.

Cumloquoy was very reticent subsequently about what passed between him and the captain during their interview in the cabin. It was shrewdly surmised, however, that the two men were brothers. There was not only a strong family resemblance between them, but it was remembered that Comloquoy's brother had gone south many years before, and had never returned again. It was also suspected that Cumloquoy got some money from the captain when he was in the cabin with him, and this belief was strengthened by the fact that the family were always in good circumstances afterwards.

CAUGHT AT THE "LAST"

The statement above, that the people would have taken to the hills at the first sign of danger, was in all probability too true. A story is told of a Birsay man who had lain out on the moors for weeks. At length his shoes became useless, and he went home one night to mend them. He required a light for this purpose, however, and this led to his capture. The press-gang happened to be passing the place, and the novelty of a light shining there attracted their attention. When they went up to the house they found the man whom they had been hunting after for so many weeks busy working at his shoes, and they made certain he did not escape them at that time.

A Novel Hiding Place

Those who were eluding the attentions of the press-gang, however, were not always reduced to the cold, damp heath in the glen, or to the hillside for a couch and hiding-place, as witness the case of James Flett, who hid himself in the "aitmeal kist" in Scottie, Beaquoyside, Birsay, where, it seems, he had been staying as a servant. A neighbour lass, little Mary Johnston, along with her mother, somehow got to know that the press-gang were on the prowl, and they went up to Scottie to give the alarm. Flett, whenever he got the hint, took to his hiding place in the kist; and, as the press-gang never imagined that anyone would seek shelter in the meal girnel, he escaped. Some years afterwards, Flett married the watchful wench, to whose good offices he attributed his freedom.

Mansie o' the Hause

Poor Mansie, though not living in the Hause at the time, had the misfortune to fall into the clutches of the press-gang. His mother, who was far from desirous of parting with him, gave him a very bad character to his captors. She assured them that he was not worth the trouble of taking into the town, as "he was never for use to grip a grey cuithe in his days." The press-gang, however, suspected that the description of Mansie given by his mother was scarcely an honest one, and they therefore told her it was not to grip grey cuithes they wanted him, but "to fight with sword and beggonet!"

But when Mansie reached Kirkwall he was set free by the landlord of his mother's house in Costa, Evie. The laird asked Mansie gruffly why he was not out of the way of the press-gang—away in hiding as well as the other men in the parish. No wonder the laird spoke with such a tempter to Mansie. He had to pay a good round sum of money before he could get the poor fellow clear.

BOUGHT OFF

Quite a number of men were captured under very peculiar circumstances, and were under the necessity of purchasing their freedom. William Spence, of Backs, Birsay, is an instance of this kind. He was about to be married, when he was seized by the press-gang. But, by payment of a certain sum of money, he avoided the disagreeable job of going to be "food for cannon."

George Smith in Sandwick was also impressed when a bridegroom. It happened, however, that there was a wrecked sailor in the parish at the time, and he volunteered to take the bridegroom's place on receiving the sum of forty guineas. Smith, therefore, instead of having to go to the wars, was allowed to enter the peaceful bonds of matrimony, which he much preferred. It gave the Sandwick people no little satisfaction afterwards when they learned that the sailor who took Smith's place succeeded in escaping from the service within a week or two from the time he left Orkney.

AN APPRENTICE CAPTURED

Andrew Spence, who was an apprentice joiner at Stromness, had an adventure on one occasion when passing along the road to Sandwick. He had undertaken the journey for the purpose of attending his cousin's marriage, but the press-gang pounced upon him, that he might have the honour of serving His Majesty King George on the field of battle. As young Spence had no desire to be the recipient of such an honour, he assured his captors that he could produce his "prentice indentures," and pled with them that his word might be accepted on this point, otherwise he would miss his cousin's marriage. The constables must have been in a peculiarly good frame of mind on this occasion, for they set him at liberty; so that he had the good cheer, and the "voluptuous swell" of the wedding music instead of the sounds of war and the hoarse roar of battle.

THE LAIRD OF BEAQUOY'S VICTIM

William, or Thomas, Allan was a young man living in the Beaquoyside of Birsay in press-gang times. It appears that the laird of Beaquoy was under obligation to procure a man for his property and another for his quarter of the parish. Further, he was a press-gang constable. One day he and young Allan had occasion to go the Barony side of Birsay together. As they passed along they were met by a neighbour, who asked Allan if he was not afraid to go on such a journey. To this question the youth innocently replied, "Tammie's wi' me," meaning the laird, whose name was Thomas Johnston, thus showing that he implicitly believed that his companion had the power, and would exert it, to save him from the press-gang.

When the couple reached the Barony, the authorities there asked the laird if he had got his man yet. He answered in the negative, whereupon he was questioned whether the young lad who was with him would not do. The laird indicated that he had no objection. Thereupon Allan was impressed and was not even given the opportunity of going back to his home to see his sister, who was his nearest relative alive. Thus the arm of flesh in which he trusted failed him in the dire hour of his need.

The people in the parish were much incensed at this cruel treatment of the orphan lad, and amongst some of the prayers that were put up was one that the laird might some day go out from his house as Allan did and never get back.

It was noticed that after the part that the laird played in this transaction things never seemed to go right with him; and the usage he had given to the orphan lad appeared to weigh heavily on his mind. Long ago two old Orkney dames were discussing the character of David. One of them said that "Dauvit was a good man indeed, but what did he do wi' the sodger and his wife?" So with the laird. By his instigation, young Allan was sent to the forefront of the hottest battle. But we must not judge too harshly. Money was scarce in Orkney in those days—the crofter's hen had not then begun to lay her golden eggs—and either men or money had to be provided somehow to meet the necessities of the country.

That the laird had some qualms of conscience for what he had done was abundantly proved by his kindness to Allan's sister. He took that young woman to reside with him at Beaquoy, and kept her there till she died.

At length the prayers of the parish were realised. The laird was seen setting out for Stromness one day, "greeting" as he went. He was going away there for the purpose of bonding his property. When he arrived at the house of John Copland, in Stromness, he took ill and shortly afterwards died there, so that, like Allan, he left his home and never returned.

As for Allan, after "the peace," he became a waterman at an English port, but he never came back to Orkney. A Birsay man met him once, when he said he was going to write to the laird, but by that time Johnston had been gathered to his fathers.

SUCCESSFUL MALINGERING

Many anecdotes are told of the tricks adopted by those who were captured by the press-gang to escape service. A few samples of these may be given.

Walter Rossie, who belonged to Stroma, happened to be at Flotta one day, when he was captured by the press-gang. He was a strong, healthy-looking man, and was considered by his acquaintances to be very clever. When he was put on board ship he at once began to play the fool. Every means that could be thought of was used for the purpose of trying to get Rossie to commit himself, without avail. At last the captain of the vessel took him in hand. He handed Rossie a silver coin and asked him what he would do with it. The malingerer took the coin in his hand, turned it carefully over, and then declared it would make a fine "henching" stone. Pitching it flat side on the water, he clapped his hands and gleefully chuckled as he saw it bounding out of the water once or twice before it finally disappeared. That was enough for the captain. He ordered Rossie to be put ashore at once as a hopeless fool.

A man from the township of Hourston, Sandwick, after being taken to Leith, feigned deafness. He was examined by doctors, and was tested in many ways, but he played the role of the mute so successfully that he, too, was made happy in being ultimately sent home as of no use for active service.

Another Sandwick man who was captured by the press-gang pretended that he was a victim to epilepsy, and he imitated the fits so well that he was considered of no use for His Majesty's service, so that he was also returned to his native county.

SAVED BY GREY CUITHES

John Tait, a native of Holm, had a perfect terror of the press-gang. One night he was standing at the end of his house when he saw in the distance two men coming in his direction, whom he suspected to be constables. He fled for refuge to the barn, and was speedily followed by the members of the press-gang. The constables overturned everything in the place, but could not find their man. They remained about the farm all night however, in the hope that they might get hold of Tait, but in the morning they had to leave, being quite baffled. Whenever they were clear of the place Tait dropped down from the cupplebacks of the barn, where he had been forced to sit for so many hours. A few days afterwards the constables returned to the farm. They came upon the scene so suddenly that Tait had not time to get out to his old place of concealment, so that he took refuge in the corn-chest, placing a piece of pipe shank under the lid in order to give him a little air. Again he escaped, but he saw he was being watched so closely that sooner or later he would fall into the clutches of his pursuers. He therefore commenced dieting himself largely on raw grey cuithes, with the result that eruptions came out all over his body. At length he was caught, but when he was examined by a doctor he was declared unfit for service. In after years, when recounting his experiences with the press-gang, Tait was in the habit of declaring that it was the grey cuithes which saved him.

A BIG RISK

Two men belonging to Holm were one day walking along the banks at Roseness Point, when they saw the press-gang approaching. The constables had so arranged themselves that the men were hemmed down on the point. At that place there is a dangerous crag known as the Doo Cot, and one of the men threw himself over the cliffs, at the Swing, and began clambering down the face of the almost perpendicular rocks. His companion, seeing that this was their only hope of escape, soon followed suit. After a terrible struggle both men reached the Cot in safety, and there was not a man in the press-gang who had the courage to go down the cliffs to attempt dislodging them. The constables thought they would manage to starve the men out, but they failed. It happened to be the nesting time, and the man got any quantity of sea-birds' eggs with which to sustain themselves, and ultimately their friends in the parish, hearing of the predicament they were in, got a number of women to go to their rescue. The fair sex armed themselves with sticks and stones and succeeded in driving the constables away from the place. A rope was then lowered to the men and they were safely hoisted to the banks again, being little the worse of their terrible experience on the cliffs.

THE RED WAISTCOAT

One day the press-gang was seen coming to Holm from the direction of Deerness. The signal went like wild-fire over the whole parish, so that very soon there was not a man to be seen anywhere. It was quite evident to the press-gang that their arrival had been announced, but they passed on as if they had no intention of making a seizure. The people in the west end of the parish watched the constables disappear to the westward as if making for Kirkwall, and were delighted to think that the residents in Holm were to escape their attention. In the course of an hour or so, believing danger was past for the present, the men commenced to leave their hiding-places. They were beginning to congratulate themselves on the narrow escape they had made when they observed a man with a red waistcoat walking leisurely up the Warthill, and immediately behind him a few companions. The tailor of Gyers always wore a red waistcoat, and it was concluded that it would be he, accompanied by some Deerness men. Tailors as a rule may be depended upon for being Radical, and in sympathy with the feelings of the people; and he of Gyers was no exception in this respect. He was never done denouncing the press-gang and wanting to know why the lairds and big tenants were not forced to go and fight the French as well as poor people. Thus the tailor of Gyers was looked upon as a friend, and as one who could be depended on to help to humbug the press-gang. The red waistcoat had therefore little terror for those who had been hiding from the constables; but to make sure that there was no mistake in the matter, two young unmarried men volunteered to go up to the Warthill to reconnoitre. They did so, but never returned. One of the press-gang, knowing that the tailor of Gyers was a favourite with the people, had donned a red-coloured waistcoat, and the other constables had also disguised themselves so well that the young men already referred to were completely taken in, and were easily captured. The names of these two victims were John Gorn and William Bruce, and the fact that the incident is remembered in detail, indicates the feeling of the parishioners on the subject.

A KINDLY INTENTION FRUSTRATED

Old Oddie of Cornquoy, Holm, had a servant whom the members of the press-gang had been instructed to apprehend. Oddie was one of the constables, and he had such a liking for his servant lad that he gave him the hint to go into hiding. The young man went to Muckle Occlester, a distance of about two miles. After being there some time the press-gang came to hear of his whereabouts. The whole force of constables therefore went up to that farm to have a search for him. After making sure that he was not in the dwellinghouse, they proceeded to the barn. One of the constables noticed that Old Oddie was poking his stick amongst a bundle of heather "simmons" in a most gingerly way. "Man, Oddie," said the constable, "you're pushing your stick amongst that heather as if ye thocht it covered a lot of eggs. Let's see it." So saying, he took the stick from Oddie and sent it amongst the simmons with such force that the servant lad gave an "Oh!" and started to his feet. He was, of course, captured and carried away from his native home; but he had a kindly feeling for his master, because he knew he tried not to discover his hiding-place amongst the heather. When opportunity occurred, he returned to his native parish and was always on good terms with those at Cornquoy.

AN INTERRUPTED COURTSHIP

John Garrioch, a Holm man, was in love with the daughter of one of the press-gang constables. One night he went away to see his lady-love and found her in tears. On asking an explanation, she told him the press-gang had got orders to apprehend him and send him off to the wars. That he might be taken by surprise, it had been resolved to capture him that night; and very likely at that very moment the constables might be at his house. After discussing matters with his sweetheart, it was agreed that he should go and sleep in a neighbour's house, where it was considered unlikely that the press-gang would go. Garrioch went to the house agreed upon, but he had not had time to get asleep when he heard a loud knocking at the door. He suspected that this was the enemy, so slipping on his trousers and vest he rushed to the other side of the passage. When the constables entered the house they made direct for the room where he had been sleeping, whilst he quietly made his exit. He sped to the hills, half-naked as he was, and remained their in that condition all night. About ten o'clock next morning he met an old woman, who kindly lent him a petticoat and shawl, and in this disguise he went home and partook of breakfast. Subsequently he went out and lay down in a field of oats near to his own house. But it got tiresome lying there a whole day, and in the afternoon he cautiously raised his head to see if the coast was clear, so that he might get into the house for some food. The press-gang had suspected that he would choose this field of oats as a suitable hiding-place, and they had been watching it from a distance through a spyglass. The moment he lifted his head he was seen and the constables pounced upon him and took him prisoner. A capture of this kind always raised the ire of the women folk, and more than the usual amount of sympathy was shown to Garrioch owing to the fact that he was on the eve of being married. Amongst those who surrounded the constables, volubly expressing their opinion of such conduct, were Garrioch's sister and sweetheart, and they marched more than half way to Kirkwall with him. Ultimately Garrioch was allowed an opportunity to bid his sweetheart good-bye. The parting was a sorrowful one, but vows were taken on the road, and in presence of the press-gang, that were never broken. After the war was over Garrioch returned to his native parish and found that his sweetheart had remained true to him. There was a wedding, and perhaps it was all the more enjoyed after the long and wearisome separation.

A MIDNIGHT SEARCH

In press-gang times peaceable people were never certain of a night's rest. The constables selected the midnight hour as peculiarly suitable for making captures, and often went the round of a parish through the night looking for victims. On one occasion they surrounded a house in which a young man named Brass was residing, and demanded admittance. Brass knew quite well that he was the man wanted, so he rose from his bed, and the moment the door was opened he bolted, having no clothing on but his shirt. One of the constables made a grab for Brass, and actually got a handful of his nether garment. The press-gang set off in pursuit of the young fellow, but after a chase of three miles they had to give in. Meantime Brass reached the house of a friend where he was clothed and congratulated on having such a narrow escape, though he had caused something of a sensation on presenting himself for protection practically garbless.

INGENUITY REWARDED

John Stanger, a young man belonging to the West Mainland, had a stirring adventure with the press-gang. The constables had captured him out in the Birsay district and were conveying him to Kirkwall that he might be examined by a doctor, preparatory to being sent off to join the army or navy. When they were crossing a burn in Harray, however, he stumbled and apparently sprained his foot so badly that he could not walk. The press-gang declined to carry him, and so they "kugged" and hauled time about at his foot in order to get it set. After the constables had expended much time and force on these operations, young Stanger professed that he was a little better, and he was able to limp along with his captors to Finstown. Here the press-gang went into a house for refreshments and to secure a horse to carry their lame prize to Kirkwall. Whilst they were enjoying themselves drinking, young Stanger limped to the door to get a mouthful of fresh air. By and by the constables thought he was staying outside too long, and when they went in search of him, their disgust may be imagined when they observed the supposed cripple spanking like a deer up the hills above Finstown! Stanger had got such a long start, and was going over the ground at such a tremendous pace that the constables concluded it was hopeless to go off in pursuit of him. Nothing therefore remained for them now but to march into the metropolis, which they forthwith did, sadder and wiser men. As for their prize, whose foot was so suddenly cured, he sought at his leisure "his home in the west," his return being a delightful surprise to his friends, who had made up their minds that there was no hope of his escape, and who fully expected when he was taken away that they had parted with him for years, if not for ever.

CAPTURED BY TREACHERY

Three men who were wanted by the press-gang were hidden away in the old kirk at Holm. Arrangements were made by their friends whereby the beadle of the church would be able to carry food to them at stated intervals, and in a way that would not raise the suspicions of the constables. The plan wrought beautifully for a week or two, and hopes were being entertained that they were going to escape. But a man named David Spence seems to have had a spite against one or more of the fugitives, and he, getting hold of the secret, informed the authorities, and the whole lot were captured. The people were so indignant at Spence for his treachery that he was glad to get out of the parish with a whole skin, and he volunteered to join the service himself, getting £40 for so doing. In the course of the war he was captured by the enemy, and spent nearly four years in a dismal French prison; but was subsequently released, and returned home.

A FEMALE SPY

William Ritch, of the Kitchen, Holm, was one of the press-gang constables, but he was not a great success. No matter how privately he made his arrangements for going out to capture young men for the service, they seemed to know of his approach, and he could never get even within hailing distance of anyone who was wanted. If he had applied to his wife for an explanation, however, she could have given it. She was a kindhearted old woman, and her sympathies were all in favour of the people and against the press-gang. Accordingly, whenever she saw her husband making arrangements for a raid she dispatched one of her boys to the neighbouring houses to give warning, with the result that all serviceable men took to the cliffs or to the hills till the danger was past.

Taking Refuge in Stroma

It is said that in press-gang times strangers visiting the island of Burray would have thought that it was inhabited by women alone. Not a man was to be seen. Those who remained at home went about in women's clothing, and the others, whenever a small boat containing strangers was observed in the vicinity, either proceeded to sea or set off for another island. One day the press-gang were seen approaching. A heavy sea was running in Holm Sound at the time, this being caused by a gale blowing in the face of the tide. Three men who suspected they were the parties who were wanted—Thomas Sinclair, David Foubister and James Banks—immediately manned a boat and set off for the island of Stroma. They reached their destination in safety, and whether the press-gang had got a fright crossing Holm Sound or whether they really did not know where the men had gone, is not known; but they did not go further than Burray, so that they did not succeed in making a capture.

Caught!

Harry Wylie and Solomon Guthrie, two men belonging to the island of Burray, were out fishing one day when they saw a boat leaving St Mary's with the press-gang. The Burray men, in the hope that they had not been seen, ran their boat ashore on Glimps Holm, turned it upside down and got underneath to await developments. By and by, when the press-gang boat was passing the little island some of the constables noticed the upturned boat, and it was thought worth while going ashore to investigate. The members of the press-gang on turning up the boat were delighted to find the two Burray men. They were ordered to get to their feet, and to consider themselves prisoners. Harry Wylie slowly rose from the ground, and as he did so it was discovered that he had a club foot, and was therefore useless either as a soldier or a sailor. Solomon Guthrie was next examined, when it was seen that the poor man had a wooden leg. It is needless to add that the press-gang would not take a gift of either; and when they found on going to Burray that there was not a man on the island, they could not help thinking that Wylie and Guthrie had acted the part of decoy birds, so as to give their friends time to make their escape.

A CURE FOR JAUNDICE

John Wards, a Stromness man residing at Burray, had the misfortune to fall into the hands of the press-gang. Afterwards, in the course of an engagement with the French, he was taken prisoner. During the time he was in the French prison he had a severe attack of jaundice, of which he was cured by an old French woman. The medicine which he got was made from the juice of herbs, and he prevailed upon the old woman to give him the recipe for making it. After he returned to Burray he cured several people of jaundice with the same medicine, but he would never give up the secret of how it was made. On his death-bed, however, he gave the information to his daughter, and she guarded the secret as carefully as her father had done. The cure was said to have a wonderful effect upon sick people. It was known in Burray as the French cure for jaundice.

A STRONG MAN

A man named Harcus, belonging to Tankerness, had some very narrow escapes with the press-gang. On one occasion he was hotly pursued in his own parish, and only escaped by scrambling down the face of the cliffs and secreting himself in one of the caves at the Point of Ness. The constables knew Harcus would, sooner or later, be driven from his hiding-place by hunger, and they kept therefore a strict watch in the vicinity. One night Harcus slipped out of the cave and crept up to a neighbour's house for rest and refreshment. A constable, however, happened to see him and cautiously followed him in every movement that he took. The result was that Harcus was taken from bed and conveyed to Kirkwall. When the press-gang arrived at Cromwell's Fort in Kirkwall they flashed a light that a crew might be sent ashore from a man-of-war vessel which was then in the bay. The signal, however, was not observed, so that the press-gang resolved to secure a small boat and take their prisoner out to the vessel themselves. As the craft left the shore the men noticed that it was leaking, but they thought it would keep afloat long enough for their purpose. When half way out to the frigate, Harcus, who was a very strong man, laid his shoulders to one side of the boat and his feet to the other, giving such a terrific jerk that he displaced a number of planks. The boat almost immediately began to fill and it sank within a few minutes Three of the members of the press-gang were drowned, but Harcus succeeded in swimming ashore and escaped. The incident, as might be supposed, caused a profound sensation in the county. The authorities used every means to try and recapture Harcus, but he succeeded in getting across the Pentland Firth, and thus escaped the press-gang and the punishment which, if he had been caught, would certainly have been meted out to him for the loss of three men. Tradition has it that Harcus never returned to the county and was never heard of again.

AN EGILSAY MAN'S ADVENTURE

Hugh Hourston lived at Sound, on the west side of Egilsay, in press-gang times. He acted as an Orkney pilot and made a lot of money at the business. From his house he could see vessels whenever they entered the Westray Firth, and if they showed a Jack on their fore peak he was generally first out to see the vessel. William Craigie lived at the other side of the island, and he also acted as a pilot, but he was nearly always forestalled by Hourston and had, consequently, a bitter grudge at his successful rival. Circumstances played into the hands of Craigie, and he was supplied with the materials for having revenge on his energetic opponent. He was appointed a press-gang constable for Egilsay, and the first man that he resolved should be sent off to fight against the French was Hugh Hourston. One night Craigie got assistance from a neighbouring island, and proceeded to Sound to make his capture. When he came to the door, however, he was refused admittance. Hourston had suspected what was in the wind, and

he made arrangements for "running up the flag"—in other words, he resolved to remove a flag at the back side of the roof, and while his sisters were holding the constables in check at the door he quietly left the premises, put off with his little boat and proceeded to Rousay. At length the constables forced

the door open, but by that time the bird had flown, the flag had been replaced, and there was no clue left behind as the direction which Hourston had taken. The constables were so angry at losing their man that they used abusive language to Hourston's sisters, who retaliated by attacking the discomfited officers. For several nights in succession the officers returned to the house and ranselled it, but without effect. A week or two afterwards, Hourston returned to the island, and Craigie, hearing of this, laid plans with much care so as to secure a capture. An innocent-looking frigate came down the Westray Firth, showing a Jack for a pilot, and Hourston put out to it quickly followed by Craigie. By the time Hourston had begun to suspect the character of the vessel he was approaching, a small boat had been sent off for his capture. With the constables behind him and the bluejackets in front, he had no chance of escape, and was speedily made a prisoner. Immediately after he was put on board the vessel it went across the Pentland Firth to Scrabster, to receive some men who had been impressed in Caithness. After this, the frigate returned to Orkney, but when going through Hoy Sound it was in danger of being lost owing to a sailing-master being unacquainted with the tides. At this juncture, Hourston offered to pilot the vessel into harbour at Stromness, and his services were gladly accepted. The captain of the frigate was so grateful to Hourston for bringing the vessel into port in safety, that he gave him liberty to go ashore. This was the chance which Hourston never expected to get, and it was too good not to be embraced. When he landed in Stromness he proceeded to a friend's house, where he went into hiding, and remained there till after the vessel had left the harbour. Shortly afterwards a schooner required the services of a pilot to get through the Westray Firth. Hourston got this job, and was landed at Egilsay. Before he left this vessel, however, he told the captain of the way he had been captured, and expressed his fears that he might be again caught. The captain, sympathising with Hourston, gave him a cutlass and pistol, telling him at the same time that if the press-gang interfered with him he was not to be afraid to use these weapons in his own defence. Hourston was a powerful fellow, and when it became known amongst constables that he was armed, he was not again molested. Subsequently he went to sea and he escaped altogether from having to serve either in the army of the navy. It was supposed that the captain of the man-of-war vessel had let Hourston ashore at Stromness to give him the chance of escaping as a reward for having saved his ship from disaster in Hoy Sound.

After many subsequent attempts to capture Hourston, Hugh McLauchlan, one of the soldiers then stationed in Kirkwall, was sent out with a boat's crew to search the island, as also a wind-bound vessel then lying in the Sound between Rousay and Egilsay in which it was thought he might be hiding, their orders being to bring him in dead or alive. Not finding him in the island they went to the vessel. Upon presenting their instructions to the captain, he replied, "You are at liberty to search my ship. You will not find him here; he is on that island," pointing to Rousay, "and your instructions do not call you there to look for him. So if you want to be clear of a dirty job you will return to Kirkwall, as you have now fulfilled your instructions." This they were not sorry to do. McLauchlan used to say that it was with very bad will he set out on that morning's job, but as a soldier he dared not disobey orders.

TWO BROTHERS PRESSED

In press-gang times the island of Rousay was owned by Mr Baikie of Tankerness. The laird and some of the principal tenants held a meeting to fix upon the men who should be sent off to the war as representatives of Rousay, when, amongst others, David Mowat was selected. Arrangements were made so secretly for the capture of the victims that they were carried out most expeditiously and with great success. Mowat was very indignant at the way he had been treated, and when on the passage from Rousay to Kirkwall he maintained a sulky silence; but he was probably ruminating on how he should get quits with those who had been the means of tearing him from his home. At that time large numbers of people gathered down at Kirkwall harbour daily to await the arrival of the press-gang boats, so as to see who the victims might be.

Amongst those at the harbour that day was Colonel Balfour. Mowat rushed over to him and volunteered to serve for Shapinsay. Colonel Balfour was delighted to get his services, and assured him that if he returned safe from the war he would never want for a farm. The laird of Rousay and his friends were very wroth at being deprived of their man in this simple way, and arrangements were made to capture John Mowat— David Mowat's youngest brother.

Colonel Balfour seems to have got a hint of this, for next day, when the press-gang boat arrived from Rousay he was again there, and told the officers that the war was not yet so hot that they were reduced to taking two members from the same family. Without further palaver he ordered John Mowat to be taken back to his native island, and his influence was such in the county, that he was instantly obeyed. By the time David Mowat had arrived at Portsmouth, the news of the great victory at Waterloo had been received in this country, and he, along with many others who had been impressed for the service, were therefore allowed to return home. Though Mowat had never been to the war, Colonel Balfour faithfully redeemed his promise by giving his a snug little farm in Shapinsay.

OLD ORKNEY HOUSES

As people often found hiding-places in their own houses, it may be well to describe here the general appearance of these. Young folk have little idea nowadays of the sort of houses their forefathers lived in. They were, with few exceptions, one-storeyed and had thatched roofs. When the buildings were exposed to westerly gales, what was known as a "gavock" was erected on the lower end of the close between the byre and the stable. The door of the firehouse was used also as the entrance to the byre. A wall, called the "cattie wa'," separated the "ca'esneuk" from between the doors. Over this porch and the place where the calves were kept, pieces of wood were placed, and this was called a "hallan," and was used for storing caisies and similar articles. Between the side of the house and the inner door space was left for a "peat-neuk," and over this the quern, or hand-mill, generally stood on a bench. The fire was situated on the middle of the floor, and the smoke had to pass out through a hole in the roof called the lum.

HIDING-PLACES IN DEERNESS

The people of Deerness had numerous places for concealing themselves from the press-gang. Among these may be mentioned Eunson's cave in the cliff below Stonehall, the caves in Burry Geo and Lang Geo, a peculiarly-shaped place called the Repenting-Stool at the Banks of Helley, and the Holes in the Horn. Another hiding-place was the Hole in the Brough. This is an artificial passage from the old buildings to the top of the cliff. So many men were there at one time that the air became vitiated, and some of them narrowly escaped with their lives. The Smuggler's Cave in the Geo of Swinnapull, where a smuggler subsequently landed his cargoes of illicit goods from his vessel, and then had the kegs tied up in winlans of straw and carted into Kirkwall, was also a special resort for those who were hiding from the press-gang, as it could only be approached by water.

One day Robert Matches, Horris, Deerness, was just emerging from the close of his house when he saw the press-gang within two hundred yards of him. He at once fled into the house, but the officers were so near that they saw him and were quite sure that they would have an easy capture. When they entered the house, however, Matches could not be found. Every nook and cranny in the place was carefully searched, and the constables had at length to admit that they were completely baffled. Ultimately, when they left Horris they were half under the impression that it must have been a wraith they had witnessed. No sooner were they at a safe distance from the place, however, than signal after signal was given to Matches by his friends that the coast was clear, but to their surprise he made no reply. At last, getting alarmed, some of them went under the bed and raised a flagstone, when it was found that the unfortunate man had gone down into the hole so suddenly that he had not left the smallest space to give himself air, with the result that he was perfectly unconscious, and it took a considerable time to revive him. Matches afterwards stated that the agony he endured prior to becoming unconscious was such that he would never again go into the same hiding-place.

BETRAYED BY A CHILD

David Cromarty, Northhouse, Deerness, was sitting smoking at his own fireside one day, when his wife gave the alarm that the press-gang were approaching the house. David, as a provision for an eventuality of this kind, had taken the precaution of removing the shelves from a press so as to give him a handy hiding-place, and he at once rushed into it. When the press-gang entered the house Mrs Cromarty was busily engaged at the spinning-wheel, and she put on such a bold front that the constables began to suspect that their man had made good his escape. In reply to a question, Mrs Cromarty invited the press-gang to search the premises if they though her husband was on them. Her little two-year-old child, whose pet name was "Davick," was playing at her feet whilst the press-gang were searching the hallan and the peat-neuk for Cromarty, and he clapped his hands in glee as he saw them going every where but the right place. At last, when they were on the point of leaving, the little child, anxious to show off his knowledge, shouted "Da's in dae press." The mother tried to drown his voice, but this only had the effect of making him more determined to let it be known where his father was, and he finished up by pointing to the cupboard. Acting on the hint so persistently given by the child, the members of the press-gang opened the door and placed the baton on Cromarty's shoulder. As they hurried away to Kirkwall with the poor man they were followed by his weeping wife. When they had got as far as Windbreck, one of the members of the press-gang, taking pity on the sorrowful wife, tried to pacify her by saying, "Dunno greet, Sarah, for while I hae a bannock thu'll aye get a half o't." The poor woman did not get much comfort from the promise; and it was only at the express desire of her husband that she was at last prevailed upon to bid him farewell and to return to her now desolate home. Next day she was sitting sadly crooning the air of Martyrdom and thinking of her hard lot, when little Davick gave a joyful scream and cried, "Oh, ma, there's da at dae window." In an instant the mother was at the door and was in the arms of her husband. It then transpired that when Cromarty was examined by the doctor his legs were found to be all scarred and burnt, so that he was declared unfit for service. Cromarty had, it turned out, rubbed his legs with vitriol; but they were so long in healing and the pain was so intense that he declared nothing would induce him to try a similar trick again.

A Dead Shot

As a rule, the press-gang preferred single men to married. Andrew Delday, who lived at Holland, Deerness, was in many respects a very suitable party for press-gang purposes. Though only seventeen years of age, he was tall and muscular—being over six feet in height. In fact, he is said to have been taller by several inches than any other man in the parish, and our informant says that "his equal has not been seen in Deerness since he left it." He had one drawback, however—we mean for the press-gang—"he was fearless and had a determined bearing," so that the constables were afraid to tackle him. He had a gun, too, which he carried about with him continually, and he always declared that the man who tried to capture him should get its contents at short range. One night after he had retired to his bed-chalmer (this was the title given in those days to a room which was generally erected on the opposite side of the close from the principal dwellinghouse, for the use of the grown-up members of the family), he was aroused by hearing a noise as if someone was trying to force the door. He demanded to know who was there, but got no reply. Thinking he might have been mistaken, he was slowly dozing off to sleep again when the noise was repeated. Being now thoroughly aroused, he ordered the aggressor to speak or he would fire at him. Again he got no reply, and so he rose and examined the fastenings of the door to make sure that they were all right. Once more he retired to bed, only to be again disturbed. His patience being now exhausted, he fired his gun, aiming low, so as, he said, to make sure that he should wound, but not kill, his tormentor. The shot effectually put a stop to the disturbance, and Andrew was allowed to spend the remainder of the night in peace. Next morning, however, he was aroused by hearing his sister excitedly shouting at his door. Hastily dressing and going outside, he found the cause of all the commotion the previous night was an old ewe, which was lying in the close dead, having been shot through the heart. With a rueful countenance he explained how the thing had occurred, but he had reason to regret his outspokenness, for his sister immediately began to chaff him on the brave defence he had made against an old sheep. The story speedily spread over the parish, and though the men dared not mention the matter to him it was different with the fair sex. They persecuted him so mercilessly about killing the old ewe that at last he took packet for Leith, determined to put some miles of sea between himself and his fair tormentors. The vessel was driven back by stress of weather to Holm Sound, however, and he crossed over to Deerness to see his friends, in the hope that his short absence might have softened their hearts. But in addition to the story regarding the sheep, he found he had now to face their jeers about his short voyage, so that once more he left his native parish, declaring that he should never return to it again. A few months afterwards he reached London, where the press-gang, consisting of ten men, tried to capture him, but in vain. At last, growing weary of the continuous anxiety to elude the press-gang, he joined the navy of his own accord, and was speedily promoted to the rank of boatswain on a corvette. But he got disgusted at the frequency with which he saw the men being flogged, and he ultimately deserted. Many years afterwards he was seen in London by a lady from Deerness, and he was then in easy circumstances. Even then, however, he had such a lively recollection of the chaffing he had been subjected to over "the dead shot," that he said he would never again return to his native parish, and he kept his vow.

"HE'S GONE"

William Delday, Deerness, was working in the vicinity of his father's farm one day when he got the signal that the press-gang were approaching. As he emerged from the stackyard he almost ran into the arms of his would-be captors. Suddenly throwing his arms out on either side of him, however, he speedily cleared the members of the press-gang out of his way, and rushed off in the direction of the Mull Head. His pursuers, believing that there was no chance of escape for him, followed closely. Upon reaching the cliffs, Delday, without the slightest hesitation, bounded right over. When the press-gang came up to the place, hot and breathless, they could find no trace of their man. As they stood gazing over the heights they heard a tremendous splash, and immediately afterwards a large volume of spray leapt up the cliffs. The members of the press-gang mutely looked at each other, but their demeanour plainly showed that they had all arrived at the same conclusion—Delday had drowned. Upon their return from the Mull Head, Delday's father demanded to know what they had done with his son. For a time they would give no answer, but at length one of them, with a shake of the head, which told even more than his words, whispered, "He's gone." The story of the accident was afterwards told in detail and caused a great sensation in the parish. Two nights afterwards, Delday's father gathered his children around the fireside to engage in family worship. He had announced for the lesson the 1st chapter of Job, and was turning over the leaves of his Bible looking for the place, when the attention of the family was arrested by a hurried footstep in the close. "That's Willie's footstep." whispered the mother, and all eyes were at once turned to the door. The next moment he was in the house, surrounded by his sorrowing friends who looked upon him as if he had returned from the grave. The explanation of his mysterious disappearance at the Mull Head was soon given. Shortly before, he had been down the cliffs there hunting for sea-fowls' eggs, and therefore knew the place so well that he thought he would risk the descent rather than fall into the hands of the press-gang. He got down in safety to within a yard or so of the water, when the ledge of rock on which his feet were resting gave way and went splashing into the sea. Retaining a hold of the rock with his hands, he swung along till he got a fresh foothold, and, having rested himself there for a time, he began the ascent. When he got above, his pursuers had gone away, and he then proceeded to Lang-geo, a place which had hitherto been known as an otter's hole. Removing some large stones from the entrance he was delighted to find a beautiful cave. Stalactitic and stalagmitic formations of dazzling beauty glowed all around him in the light admitted by the passage through which he had crawled. Here he lay concealed for two days, living on limpets. Afterwards, Delday joined the mercantile marine, and a few years subsequently transferred his services to the navy. Having distinguished himself in the capture of some prizes he was promoted to captain of the foretop. Before he had drawn his prize-money, however, he was killed by a fall on board his ship. His brother received the necessary documents, and employed a party to make application to the Admiralty for the prize-money, but the family never got it.

A Press-Gang Mark

The man who was looked upon as the greatest hero in Deerness in press-gang times was Andrew Paplay. The constables had searched for weeks for him, and one day they saw him at the west end of the parish. As they had their man well in view, they set off in pursuit. Paplay, who was swift of foot, went off at a smart pace in the direction of Holm, and by the time he reached Graemeshall he had so far out-distanced his pursuers that he though he could risk going in there, where he was sure of getting refreshments from his sister. He was put into a garret, where he found that there was a Holm man also in hiding. After getting some food and a rest his spirits revived, and he then said that he would rather put to sea than remain at Graemeshall to be trapped like a rat in a hole. He therefore got his sister persuaded to go down to the beach and assist him in launching a boat. The moment he put off, however, he was discovered by the press-gang, who manned a boat and followed him in hot haste. Paplay handled the oars so well that he was quite maintaining his start, till he got beyond Lamb Holm when he met with an unfortunate accident—one of his oars snapped, and he saw he would have to resort to strategy if he was to escape. He therefore slipped into a cave. When the press-gang came up to the place they suspected what had happened and succeeded in capturing their man. They took Paplay's boat in tow and made back towards Graemeshall as speedily as possible.

Having beached their own boat, the press-gang ordered Paplay to come ashore. Upon getting this command, Paplay picked up the broken oar which was lying in his boat and dashed amongst his captors. He struck one of them named Mansie Budge such a blow on the nose that it laid him low. As Paplay was courting the sister of the other constable (William Stove), he though he had nothing to fear from him. He was rushing past that individual with a friendly nod, and it looked as if he were to get clear away, when Stove tripped him and threw him to the ground. Before he could regain his feet he was again seized, and was in course of time conveyed to Kirkwall. Captain Gourlay, who received all the men whom the press-gang brought to Kirkwall, when he was told of the mauling which Budge had received, asked Paplay, "What made you kill the man?" Paplay's prompt reply was, "My manly heart, sir!" Meantime, Paplay had been brooding over the wrong which had been done to him by his sweetheart's brother, and he determined to be revenged on him. Accordingly he enlisted and offered, if allowed to visit his own parish before being sent south, to capture a suitable man for His Majesty's service. Paplay was allowed on these terms to return to Deerness, when he secured Ned Stove, brother of William Stove, whom we have just referred to. This was diamond cut diamond; but Ned Stove's indentures were got in from Stromness in time to effect his liberation. As things turned out, Paplay never had to engage in active service. By the time he reached Leith, news was received that Napoleon had been captured, and Paplay was allowed to return home. As for

Mansie Budge, he carried to the grave the mark of the blow which he received from Paplay. A growth, said to be as large as a potato, accumulated on the point of his nose, which was always pointed to as the press-gang mark.

SAD END TO A DEERNESS HEROINE

One day a large vessel hove-to off the Mull Head of Deerness and hoisted a signal indicating that a pilot was required. In response a crew of four men—James Spence, Thomas Irvine, Robert Stove, and Magnus Ritch—at once put off to offer their services. As they neared the ship, however, they began to suspect that she was a war-vessel in disguise, and they therefore resolved to make for the shore as speedily as possible. The moment the Deerness men put about, a boat manned by blue-jackets shot round the off side of the disguised cruiser. A most exciting race then ensued. Though the natives had fewer oars, they knew the tidal currents better than their pursuers, and therefore managed for a time to retain their lead. Two young women—Barbara Wick and Barbara Dinnie—having noticed the contest, at once concluded what it meant. They therefore threw aside their cards and spinning-wheels and rushed to the cliffs, gathering a lapful of stones apiece as they ran. As the boats were some distance off they continued to gather until they had quite a collection of stones. Barbara Wick then took her stand at the top of the Gate, as it was called, and eagerly watched the close of the exciting race. In the Deerness boat was her avowed lover, and she was resolved that he should not be captured if she could prevent it. The man-of-war boat, after getting through the tideway, was gradually gaining on the Deerness boat, and sometimes it looked as if it were impossible for the men to land and get up the cliffs in time to escape. Barbara, who was watching the race with breathless anxiety, seeing her friends hesitate, as if not sure where to find a landing place, in a loud voice directed them to a safer geo. As they sprang ashore they were assisted by the intrepid woman, and as they crawled up the crags she boldly covered their retreat. As soon as the Deerness men had got safely over the rocks, Barbara turned and faced the foe alone. Whenever the sailors landed and tried to mount the crags they were assailed by a shower of stones. The moment a tar tried to move upwards, a stone was sent flying towards him with unerring aim, with the result that the woman was able for a long time to hold the passage. By and by, however, her supply of stones ran out and one of the sailors made a dash at the woman. Taking her in his arms he attempted to use liberties with her. But Barbara was as strong as she was bold, and she succeeded in hurling her assailant down the pass upon his comrades, so that they were all precipitated to the beach in a struggling mass. After that the sailors returned to their ship, but it was never known what injuries they had received. One of the men thus rescued, having lost his sweetheart by death, sought and secured the hand of Barbara Dinnie, and the two spent a happy married life of upwards of fifty years. Barbara Wick, however, received a poor return for her heroism. Her lover, notwithstanding all that she had done for him, trifled with her affections and she left the parish in disgust. Subsequently, she joined her fortunes with a travelling merchant who had come to Orkney to do business at the great Lammas Market. This did not prove a happy match, and Barbara taking her two children with her set out to look for a new home. With her own hands she built a house on a lonely hillside in Caithness, and kept herself and children alive by going to the fishing. Some mischievous lads, however, pulled the maintree out of the house and the roof fell in. Barbara did not appreciate such neighbours and so she built a hut for herself in another locality. Her eldest daughter then married, and shortly afterwards her youngest child died. After this she got her little grandson to reside with her, but he was somehow killed. The poor old woman after all these misfortunes became silly. She walked the country at all hours, scolding imaginary foes, and so conducted herself that the people in the vicinity took it into their heads that she was a witch. Again the maintree was taken from her hut, and she was left without a place of shelter. The Deerness people having come to know of her sad plight, brought her back to her native parish. Here she again built a hut for herself, and the rising generation, having learned her sad history from their elders, vied with each other in providing her with comforts suitable for her old age. She lived in Deerness till she was over ninety years old, and when her end came it was peaceful.

THE PRESS-GANG IN NORTH RONALDSAY

One of the prettiest islands in Orkney during the summer months is North Ronaldsay, but in winter the tideways that surround it are often impassable for weeks on end, so that the inhabitants are very much isolated from the outer world. Looking to the situation of the island, it might have been thought that the people there would have escaped the attentions of the press-gang. But they did not. They were often called upon to supply men for the army or navy; and they had so few places in which to hide that a visit from a warship spread terror amongst young and old. One man spent a considerable amount of labour upon a cave at the west side of the island to make it a suitable and comfortable hiding-place, and he had his reward, for he was never taken. Another concealed himself in a peat-stack, and it is said that a hen used to go and lay within reach of him every morning! Be this as it may, however, he managed to elude the press-gang.

CURIOSITY PUNISHED

On one occasion a warship was seen making for North Ronaldsay, and, as may be imagined, its appearance filled the islanders with dismay. When at last the vessel dropped anchor, and a crew of bluejackets was observed pulling ashore, the people had no longer any doubt as to the object of the visit. A number of men therefore hurriedly took refuge on the Green Skerry, off Westness, and were hopeful that they would escape. At last, overcome by curiosity to see what the press-gang were doing, one of the North Ronaldsay men determined to have a peep. This was an unfortunate action both for him and his friends, for the moment he raised his head the sailors, who were then about Lennes, saw him. The islanders had no means of either offering resistance or trying to escape, as they were penned up like so many sheep, and they were all captured. Having subsequently passed the usual medical examination, they were soon afterwards forwarded to headquarters for active service.

A Hateful Summons

Cut off as the North Ronaldsay people are from the rest of the world they are very simple in their habits, and in press-gang times they were even more so than at present. At that period they looked upon the laird as a monarch whose word was law. Accordingly, when they received a summons from him to attend a meeting at Howan, they felt that they dare not disobey. They had a suspicion of what was wanted, but they feared if they did not put in an appearance at the time and place fixed upon, they might lose their crofts. The islanders therefore attended the meeting in full force, and, after some discussion, three victims were selected, viz., Thomas Tulloch, Garso; Peter Turfus, Skelperha'; and John Muir, Sheltiquoy. Though they could not possibly have escaped from the island, they were not allowed to spend their last night amongst their friends, but were locked up in the storehouse at Howan till next morning, like so many felons. They were then torn from their island homes and none of them ever returned to his native place. One of the three, however, after he got his discharge, settled down in Aberdeen, where he died.

Becalmed and Captured

The Rev. William Tulloch, minister of Westray Baptist Church, happened to pay a visit to North Ronaldsay in press-gang times. After labouring amongst the people there for a few days he proposed to return to Westray. The sea having been scanned in every direction, and there being no appearance of strange vessels in the offing, four North Ronaldsay men—two old and two young—manned a boat and started for Westray with the minister. They got becalmed, however, and were carried hither and thither with the tide. Meantime a cruiser hove in sight, and, in spite of all efforts made by the North Ronaldsay men to escape, they were captured. The two old men were not considered good enough for His Majesty's service, but the others were conveyed to Lerwick. Subsequently they were sent on to Kirkwall, but the laird of North Ronaldsay happened to see them there and he succeeded in getting a substitute for one of them, but the other was taken south and put on board a man-of-war without ever having an opportunity of saying goodbye to his friends.

A Stronsayman's Device to escape the Press-Gang

A man named Brock, belonging to Stronsay had several narrow escapes in press-gang times. One night when he had just retired to bed, the constables forced the door and entered the house, They ordered him to get up as he was now their prisoner. Brock occupied one of those old-fashioned box-beds which were so popular in those days, and he asked that he might be allowed to put on his clothes were he was. His request was granted, and he closed the doors to give himself a little privacy. His wife then began to abuse the press-gang for their hard-heartedness in taking away her husband from his poor children. At length the constables thought Brock had had ample time to dress and ordered him to leave the bed. Mrs Brock then commenced to plead with Thomas not to leave her, and the constables wishing to put and end to the painful scene threw open the doors of the bed. When they did so they got a surprise, for they discovered that their man had fled. Brock had previously loosened two boards at the back of the bed, which gave him communication with a window, and at the time he was supposed to be dressing and his wife was abusing the constables he was flying across the county on horseback, putting as great a distance as possible between himself and the press-gang. When the constables discovered how neatly they had been tricked they used some very strong language in describing what they called the hypocrisy of Mrs Brock. As for Brock himself, he got a safe hiding-place among the crags, where he remained for three weeks, being fed and attended to all the time by his friends and neighbours; and he had the satisfaction of spending the remainder of his life at home, for peace was soon afterwards declared.

AN ADVENTURE

George Reid, another Stronsay man, had one or two stirring adventures with the members of the press-gang.

On one occasion the constables surprised him in his own house. Reid at once showed fight and he succeeded in throwing two of them into the peat-fire which stood in the middle of the room, whilst the other two were laid their length on the floor. Hurrying to the beach he launched a small boat with which he made his escape to Eday. The constables, however, pursued him to that island. Again he succeeded in eluding them, and setting off to sea again, he finally landed in Walls, one of the South Isles. Once more he was attacked by the press-gang, but in such numbers that he was captured. He was put on board a war vessel, where he served for a few years. His ship having then put into an English port for repairs, he took the opportunity to desert; but this was an unfortunate move on his part, for three days afterwards peace was proclaimed. Having deserted, he of course lost his prize-money. Reid is said to have travelled from Land's End to John O'Groats on foot, and in doing so endured great hardships; but he ultimately succeeded in reaching his island home in safety.

A THREAT THAT WAS NEVER PUT IN FORCE

A Stronsay man, who was considered to be rather harmless, caused some amusement in that island in press-gang times. Whenever he knew the constables were on the hunt for men, he went to the shore, laid his legs across two stones with a space between them, and clutching a big stone in his hands loudly declared that if any attempt were made to capture him he would "snip" his legs. The fun of the thing was that the old fellow, even with his legs unbroken, would have been for no use either in the army or navy.

CAPTURE OF A FATHER AND SON

Early in press-gang times Magnus Wood, belonging to the parish of Rendall, had the misfortune to be captured. He served for some time on board a war vessel, but at length he got homesick and determined to get free of the King's service if at all possible. He had left behind him in his Orcadian home a young wife with a little baby boy, and he took a terrible heart-yearning to see them again. After thinking over several expedients he resolved that he should pretend he was deaf. At first the officers suspected that the deafness was a mere sham, but Wood played the mute so well that he at last deceived them, and was delighted to hear the captain remark to a lieutenant that he was of no use on the ship. When the vessel reached an English port Wood was discharged and lost no time in getting back to Orkney. Curiously enough, however, the war had not come to an end when Wood's son reached the age of seventeen and the youth was impressed. Young Wood had got a hint that he was wanted for service in the navy and he bolted to the hills. His sister went with him to assist in watching the movements of the constables. Night after night passed without any appearance of the press-gang, and the two got so fatigued that they resolved to go home for a night's rest. Whether the press-gang got a hint of this or not we cannot tell, but certain it is that they entered Wood's house shortly after he had retired to rest and captured him quite easily. He had only been a short time in the navy when the French war was brought to a close, and young Wood was one of the sailors sent ashore to bring off Napoleon when he was being sent as a prisoner to St. Helena. Some years afterwards Wood fell from the main-topmast of his vessel and sustained such injuries that he was discharged from the Navy on pension, which added materially to his comfort in old age.

CAPTURED AT SEA

Some Orcadians had an exciting experience one year when returning from the whale fishing at Davis Straits. They were so near home that they expected to pick up the Orkney land every moment. To their dismay, however, they discovered that they were being pursued by a British cruiser. The whaler's men persuaded their captain to put on every stitch of canvas that their vessel could stand. It soon became apparent that the cruiser was not going to catch them by sailing, but the boom of a cannon and the crash of a ball ahead of the whaler came as a warning that the latter was expected to lie to. No heed was paid to the summons, with the result that another ball came from the cruiser, which carried away the whaler's wheel, and the next shot striking the foremast just under the cross-trees the vessel became crippled. The cruiser then sent a boat to board the whaler, but the crew of the latter, with blubber knives in hand, showed fight, with the result that a second boat had to be dispatched from the war vessel. Owing to the resistance shown by the whaler's men no less than eighteen of them were taken on board the cruiser, and amongst these was a Rendall man named James Sabiston. He served in the navy for some time, and was discharged in bad health, but after he got better he was again impressed. He finally got his discharge, however, after the battle of Waterloo.

AFRAID WITHOUT CAUSE

The alarm caused by the visits of the press-gang had its humorous, as well as its pathetic side. William Scott, belonging to Rendall, was so frightened he would be captured that he hid for a whole winter in a meal girnel. He was never impressed; "but," said our informant, with a sly twinkle in his eye, "he was a poor thing and the press-gang did not think he was worth taking."

John Shurie, another Rendall man, had also great terror of imprisonment. Whenever he heard of the approach of the press-gang he put off to sea, and he always declared that before he would submit to be captured he would run into Burgar Roost—because it was as good to die in the water as to fall under the sword. John was a diminutive little fellow, far below the average height, so that he might have saved himself the trouble of rushing to sea as he would not have been accepted either as a soldier or a sailor. But he thought differently— hence his fears.

A STUBBORN DEFENCE

A man named William Harper, residing in Costa, Evie, had a stiff fight for his liberty. He had lain out in the hills for a long time hiding from the press-gang, but at last he got worn out and sought a night's shelter under his own roof. About midnight, however, the press-gang came to the door and demanded admittance. Harper at once armed himself with a three-toed pot and assumed the defensive. He warned the constables that he would use the uncouth weapon if they dared to lay hands upon him. One of the press-gang, more daring than his companions, rushed upon Harper, but he was speedily laid low. The other constables made a joint attack, but so well did Harper wield the three-toed pot that he cleared a passage for himself and set off to the hills. The constables were so badly injured in the fray that they were afraid to tackle Harper again, and he was never captured.

BROKEN-HEARTED

In press-gang times a young man belonging to Evie went out to cut peats. His sweetheart, determined that he should not be taken unawares by the press-gang, took up a position on an adjoining hill, so that she might give warning at the approach of danger. For hours she acted the part of sentinel, and was rejoiced to find that there was no appearance of the enemy in any direction. At length she thought she might venture to leave her post long enough to go home to procure some food for her lover. When she came back in sight of the peat-bank she could see no one there, but this gave her no uneasiness, as she concluded that her lover would be resting after his hard labour. As she approached the spot she began to sing a snatch of a song, but the words speedily died on her lips. Down in a hollow at the edge of the peat-bank lay her lover surrounded by the press-gang. She rushed up to the constables and pled that he might be set free. Her intercessions, however, were in vain, and in a few minutes he was led off captive. The poor girl believed that it was because she had left her watch-post that her lover had been captured, and she was so overwhelmed with grief that she died in the course of a few weeks from a broken heart. Our informant told us that he got this story from an old man who, as a boy, had been an eye-witness of the affair, and he said he never afterwards passed the spot without a feeling of sadness creeping over him.

A NOR'-WASTER'S EXPERIENCE

A man named James Johnston, who had just returned from the whale fishing at Davis Straits, was one day at the farm of Westermill, Burray, when the press-gang made its appearance. Coolly arming himself with a large plank of wood, he told the constables they were not able to take him. His aunt was there, and she had a shearing hook in her hands. Approaching the constables, she dared them to lay a finger on Johnston, threatening at the same time to test the power of her hook on their bodies. The press-gang were perfectly cowed and left their man. Johnston then crossed to South Ronaldsay and went into hiding at Stews Head. He did this, he said, not that he was afraid of being captured, but to prevent the possibility of his becoming a murderer, because he was determined there should be bloodshed rather than that he should be deprived of his liberty. He escaped and went back to the whale fishing. The whalers came to know that the man-of-war vessels lay to the eastward of Orkney awaiting their return to capture sailors, and so they passed westwards, generally landing the Orkney portion of the crew about Cape Wrath, and these poor men had to pull back, and across the Pentland Firth in an open boat. This man Johnston, along with some other Orcadians, performed this feat several times and always escaped the press-gang. At length he joined the Hudson's Bay Company as a slooper, and in this capacity he made some money. Subsequently he retired and took the farm of Mirland in Deerness, where he spent the close of his life in peace.

A HUNT BETWEEN STROMNESS AND SANDWICK

There was a Stromness man marked out for impressment, but he got a hint of it and took to his heels, out by the North End and up the Sandwick road, pursued by a constable. When he was at Consgar his pursuer was at Clumley. The hunted man's strength was ebbing fast, so he asked Mr. Tyrie to lend him a horse. Mr Tyrie said, "Tak' that young staig, and when you get whaur ye want to be juist whip the tether tae's neck and bid'm geng hame, an' he'll no lose his wey." The Stromnessian mounted the young stallion and continued his journey. Seeing this, his pursuer mounted a mare, which was tethered at Clumley, and followed as far as Quoyloo, when he was brought up in an unexpected manner "with all his sails standing." The poor mare held out till nature's utmost limit was reached, then on the Banks of Quoyloo she lay down and forthwith another horse was added to the population of Sandwick. The constable had to retrace his steps, altogether ignorant—poor man!—that in nearly every rabbit hole in his neighbourhood there was a man, at full length, watching his movements.

A Midnight Raid

F ive men acted as a press-gang in Orphir, viz., William Garrioch, Oback, Tuskabister; Nicol Wishart, Westquoy, Kirbister; John Bews, Yarpha, Smoogro; George Flett, Heathermuir, Hobbister; and George Hutchison, Suer, Clestrain. The favourite hiding-place of the men who were wanted by the press-gang was a hole at the head of Hangoback, below Gear, locally known as the Cottar Hole. It was large enough to hold from eight to ten men, and those inside could roll a large stone out to the entrance which effectually protected them from attack. William Sinclair, Gerawin, had, along with several other men in the parish, sought refuge in this place for nearly a fortnight, and during all that time their female friends slipped down in the twilight with the provisions necessary for their sustenance. As the press-gang never made a raid in the parish whilst the men were in hiding, the people began to think that they had been acting on a false alarm. Accordingly they resolved to go home to their wives and families. William Sinclair reached his house in safety and was soon comfortably bedded. But he was not destined to enjoy his night's rest in peace. Without any warning of approaching danger the door of his house was burst open, and two constables, William Garrioch and John Bews, entered. John Bews placed the baton on Sinclair's shoulder, told him he was a King's man, and without further ceremony began to pull him out of bed. Sinclair's wife, on seeing him captured, got into a dreadful state of excitement. She threw her arms round the neck of her husband and gave vent to such heart-rendering screams that Bews was filled with sympathy for her and relaxed his hold. The other constable, however, was a strong, coarse, unfeeling man. "Haud thee bye," said he to

Bews, "an' I'll no' be lang in sindering them." After a severe struggle he tore Sinclair from his wife's arms. The unfortunate man was passed by the doctor next day, and shortly afterwards was in active service. He remained on board a war vessel until peace was proclaimed, and when he returned to his native parish he was delighted to find that his wife was still alive, and they were spared to go hand in hand for many years after the war was over.

A FALSE FRIEND

Robert Ballantine, a servant lad at the Bu' of Orphir, was captured in a very treacherous way. He was on rather intimate terms with one of the press-gang constables named Nicol Wishart, and often sailed with him in his master's boat to the South Isles. Wishart was a laird's man and acted as overseer for all the kelp shores. One day he came up to Ballantine and asked him to accompany him on business to the island of Walls. As the two proceeded to the shore, Wishart told Ballantine to go over to the mill for the sails, while he himself would be getting the boat ready at the beach. Never suspecting any treachery, the servant lad proceeded to the mill, where he was surrounded by nine sailors who had been hidden there for his capture by his false friend. Ballantine was carried off to fight on board one of His Majesty's ships, was in several engagements, and after the war was over, returned to his native parish.

TWO "FOOLS"

One day when a raid was being made in the parish of Orphir by the press-gang, William Tait, Houton Head, and Andrew Clouston, News, Houton, concealed themselves in the Hole of the Heads, down on the cliffs. Their hiding-place was discovered, however, and both were captured. The men, when they saw that escape was impossible, resolved to act the fool. Tait would wander about the ship looking quite stupid-like, crying, "Did nane o' ye see Andrew o' News?" Whilst Andrew mournfully screamed that he wanted "Willock o' the Head." When they met any of the officers on deck they would try to get hold of the bright buttons which adorned their uniform, and say, "Eh, man, these are bonnie buttons. Ye might gies twa tae tak' hame tae mam." Both men wore very large jackets, and they pestered the cook "to fill their pouches wi' guid broth tae tak' hame tae mam." They were told they were to be taken to the war. "Whitna ting is hid?" asked Tait. It was explained to them that they would have to fight for their King and country. "Goth," said Clouston, "there's nae fear o' Willock o' the Head an' me fightin', is there Willock?" "Na, na," was Tait's answer: "you bonnie lads'll no' get us tae fight, I'se warran' ye for that." When they saw a bit of rope lying about the deck, they always wanted it "Hame tae tether mam's lambs wi'." The captain at last got so sick of their fooling that he dropped them off his ship at Thurso and told them with an oath to go home to their mother whom they were so continually crying about.

CAPTURED WHILST LEAVING CHURCH

Men were not safe to attend public worship in press-gang times. Peter Tait, Houar, Clestrain, was coming out of the Orphir Church one Sunday when John Bews, a constable, seized hold of him by the shoulder. Such a proceeding at once raised the ire of the female portion of the congregation, who rushed to the rescue. Mrs. Clouston, News, who took the leading part in the rescue, got hold of Bews by the arm and held on so tenaciously that Tait was able to pull himself out of his coat, which he left in the constable's hand, whilst he himself sped off up the hill. Tait was so anxious to get away that he did not speak in at his own father's house in passing, but pushed on till he reached the residence of his sweetheart in Sandwick—a distance of about twelve miles. He was never captured, "but," says our informant, "he got a wife and had a large family."

REJECTED

Thomas Tait, Culdigo, Orphir, had a deformity—a crooked finger—of which he was, curiously enough, quite proud. The press-gang pounced upon him one day and marched him to Kirkwall. It was there discovered, however, that he had this defect and he was rejected as being unfit for His Majesty's service.

A TAILOR CAPTURED

Thomas Tait, a tailor to trade, was captured in Orphir and sent off to fight the French. The enemy, in the course of a brush with the British, made a few prisoners, amongst these being Thomas Tait. For seven long years Thomas was confined in a French prison. But he was not unhappy. He ran no risk of being shot by the enemy. On the contrary, he got plenty of work to do at his trade, and when he was at length released he had a nice little nest-egg to take home with him.

WAITING ON THE WHALERS

The whalers from Davis Straits came home with such regularity and were manned with such suitable men for the navy that plans were always set to way-lay them off the Orkney coast. Old people in Orphir have some stirring stories to tell of the scenes which were witnessed in press-gang times between the whalers and His Majesty's cutters. One season Captain Gourlay, Captain Nugin, and others, were keeping a thorough lookout for the arrival of the vessels from Davis Straits. The first ship that Gourlay's cutter intercepted was about ninety miles off Cape Wrath. But the crew of the whaler suspected the work the cutter was upon, and eight of them took to a small boat as darkness was coming on, intending to return to their ship when the danger was past. Meantime, however, a thick haze set in, with the result that when they desired to return to their ship they could not find it. These poor fellows endured great hardships. They were tossed about on the sea for eight days without any food but a few biscuits; and some days they had not more than two tablespoonfuls of water. At length they were picked up in an exhausted condition by a passing vessel, and were ultimately landed in Shetland. Three of the men who had such a terrible experience in trying to elude the press-gang belonged to Orphir, viz., John Wilson, William Groundwater, and William Isbister.

The next vessel Captain Gourlay's cutter met was also a whaler, which was ordered to lay to, with yards aback. When Gourlay had reached the ship, the only one he though it worth while to take was James Snody. Upon Gourlay returning to his cutter, however, Snody had evidently volunteered the information that amongst the crew of the whaler there was a clever piper. Gourlay acted upon the hint. He returned to the whaler and declared he would not leave her till he took with him the Orphir piper. Poor Peter Sinclair, Gara, Clestrain, had therefore no option left but to accompany his captor to the cutter, and was afterwards sent off to active service.

These captures probably put Captain Gourlay in a good frame of mind, for when another whaler hove in sight and he made a demand for more men, he was told his request could not be acceded to, as most of the crew were down with scurvy. Gourlay took the word of the skipper of the whaler and did not, as usual, make a search of the vessel for himself, which was rather fortunate for some Orphir men who were on board.

A day or two later, still another whaler made its appearance. Captain Gourlay signalled to the whaler to "back her yards," but no attention was paid to this order. This exasperated Gourlay, with the result that he sent a shot flying across the bow of the whaler as an indication that if his orders were not obeyed he would sink the offender. But Gourlay got a warmer reception than he had bargained for. Instantly the whaler hove to the wind, ran out four guns and fired four shots—two before and two behind the cutter. Gourlay gave orders for the cutter to get out of range of the whaler as speedily as possible; and, as darkness soon afterwards set in the whaler received no further attention from the cutter. It turned out that the whaler was an out-of-date man-of-war vessel, and the skipper, one of the bluff old sort, determined he should not give up any of his crew without a struggle.

CONSTABLES WHO DID NOT DO THEIR DUTY

When some of the constables wanted to make a raid in Orphir it was a common custom to send a messenger, to any house from which they did not wish to take a man, on a trifling errand. This was a usual signal, and in this way the whole district was sometimes warned of approaching danger. Another method was to lay the baton on the table the day before a prowl began. This fact was soon conveyed all over the parish, and no one could say the constable who acted thus had *said* anything that could be constructed as a warning to those who were wanted.

THE LAST CLAIM ON ORPHIR PARISH

The last claim made on Orphir parish was for four men— two from Orphir, one from Swanbister and one from Houton. It was the proprietors who were applied to, and they had to find the men or pay £20. Mr. James Johnston of Coubister went up to Stromness to Captain Nugin (his brother-in-law), commander of a cutter. Two of his men enlisted and that cleared Mr. Johnston.

Then Captain Sands of Swanbister got the constables to press James Sinclair, a Swanbister lad (he was rather simple), and when he was taken to Kirkwall to be sworn in, he enlisted for Scapa, got the bounty of £20, which Captain Sands had to pay as he could not get another man.

Robert Moncrieff, proprietor of Houton and Tuskabister, could not get a man, whereupon the captain of a cutter lying in Stromness sent men down to Houton and impressed Moncrieff himself. He went along with his captors quite happy, and when he got on board the cutter he asked the commander if he though this was a manly act that he had done. Receiving no answer Moncrieff continued: "Sir, it seems to me you do not well know what you are about this morning; but when you have served you King and country as long as I have, you may come to know your duty better. However, I am willing to go if you stand the consequences." Moncrieff, however, was sent back and neither man nor money was afterwards asked.

A BIRSAY LAD'S ADVENTURE

John Johnston was born at a house called Midhouse, Beaquoyside, in the parish of Birsay, and in his lifetime was perhaps as widely known as any person in Orkney, more especially among seafaring men. He went to sea as an apprentice when very young. During his apprenticeship, however, he was impressed and put on board one of H.M. ships of war. Johnston did not at all relish his position on board a warship, and he wrote his former captain to have him released. The reply he got was that this was not in his power, but Johnston was advised to make his escape if possible, seeing he was not satisfied with his position. Johnston lost this letter from his pocket, and, strange to say, the person who found it happened to be the first lieutenant under whom he was then serving, who, of course, pretty smartly informed him that if ever he attempted to escape he would be shot on the spot. This threat, however, by no means cooled the lad's desire for freedom. Shortly afterwards he, along with other sailors, had to put some of their ship's officers ashore. It seems that the officers, before they returned, had indulged freely in drinking. When they got back to their vessel in the evening they were so far gone with drink that they did not keep a very strict watch. This was Johnston's opportunity, and, along with two other sailors, he lowered a boat. Some of the crew advised him not to try this adventure, warning him of the consequences if he were caught. Johnston's love of liberty, however, made him regardless of all danger, and he ventured ashore and made his escape, in spite of the reward offered for his capture. Had he remained in His Majesty's service he in all probability would have been quickly promoted. His smartness drew the attention of the officers, and in the very short time he was on board this vessel he was made gunner's mate. When he got clear he joined a vessel in the whale fishery business carried on at Davis Straits, which was then, and for some time after, at its best. Johnston had not been very long in this trade until he again found his way up, and very soon he was put in charge of a ship bound for Davis Straits. Captain Johnston always preferred men from Orkney as seamen and as being most suitable for those adventures connected with whale fishing. Consequently he called at Stromness every season and there engaged the greater number of his ship's crew so long as he went to sea. Captain Johnston's smartness, both as a sailor and commander, had often been admired by those who went to sea with him; and it was held that there was not a smarter captain among the whole fishing fleet. He was very successful in this business for long, and gave entire satisfaction to his employers. Indeed, it was not until he became part-owner of a whaling vessel himself that he experienced any reverse of fortune. In his vessel, Orkney men were always most numerous when going to Davis Straits, and therefore Englishmen did not have a good chance of showing their superiority to men from Orkney, as they always wished to do. Among many things of this nature, just one thing shall be noted. Those young men who were on their first voyage were termed "green hands," and it seems that some more experienced men wished to show and assert their own superiority over them. On board Captain Johnston's ship one of the inferior officers called on a very young Orkney lad when he was at his breakfast to rise and bring something. The demand was made twice, and the lad being in no hurry the officer struck him. This, of course, raised the lad's temper. He rose and challenged the aggressor, and an eye-witness testified that the officer got a complete thrashing; but no person on board ever asked that lad to do anything again, apart from his duty. Such things, of course, were unknown to the captain. The young lad referred to was from Greeny, Birsay, and was Aitken to name, and uncle to some Aitkens belonging to the West Mainland. It may be mentioned that Captain Johnston had a brother who went to Davis Straits with him, but one voyage he fell from some part of the vessel's rigging and was instantly killed.

HOW AN ORCADIAN ESCAPED FROM FRANCE

In press-gang times, William Delday, a Deerness man, was owner of one schooner and part owner of another. He had been most successful at sea, and was known as one of the pluckiest skippers afloat. But when trouble came, it was overwhelming. Delday was returning from a foreign voyage, when he was overtaken and captured by a French privateer. His courage, however, did not desert him. When he was transferred to the French vessel, Delday asked the commander what they intended doing with him. The answer he received was that as soon as he could be landed on French soil he would be cast into prison. Delday got very indignant when he was told what was in store for him and declared there was not a prison in France that would hold him. "We'll see, we'll see," sneered Monsieur, viciously twisting the ends of his moustache, and the subject dropped. When the privateer reached a French port that night it was pitch dark. This was Delday's opportunity, and he was not slow to take advantage of it. He coolly moved aft, secretly telling his men to make for the same quarter with as little noise as possible. Subsequently, when the Frenchmen were engaged stowing their sails, Delday and his men quietly dropped into a small boat which had been lowered for the purpose of landing the French captain, cut the painter and made for the Channel. It required some nerve to dodge out of the harbour unnoticed; but the adventures of Delday and his companions were only then beginning. They had neither food nor drink, and the only consolation they could find was in tobacco, of which they fortunately had a good supply. After tossing about in the Channel for twelve hours they were picked up by an

English vessel and landed somewhere in the Thames. Subsequently the other vessel in which Delday was interested was also captured, and he returned to Orkney a ruined man. His plucky escape in the face of such obstacles, and his daring in trying to cross the Channel in a small boat caused somewhat of a sensation at the time. His heroism, too, had its reward. Such representations were made on his behalf that at length a pension was secured for him, and he spent his closing years in Kirkwall. He rests under the shadow of St Magnus.

A DARING ACT

Arthur Dearness, a native of South Ronaldsay, performed one of the most daring deeds recorded in press-gang times. He was returning to this country on what, to all appearances, was to be a successful voyage. The English Channel was reached in safety, and the crew of the vessel were in high glee at the prospect of once more reaching their native shore, when, as bad luck would have it, a French cruiser hove in sight. Dearness and his crew had no chance of escape, and, in a very short time, a prize crew of Frenchmen were put on board the British vessel. The Frenchmen were in high spirits over the capture of such a well-laden merchantman, and were very insulting in their behaviour towards the British sailors. They made free with the liquors on board, and by midnight most of them were hilarious in the cabin. Dearness, being a very powerful fellow, thought the opportunity a good one for recapturing his vessel. There were only three of the French crew on deck at the time. Rushing upon these he got hold of two of them and threw one after the other into the sea. The third rushed to the cabin for safety, whereupon Dearness battened all the Frenchmen below, once more took charge of his vessel and succeeded in taking it up to the Downs, and ultimately to London. The fact that Dearness had not only recaptured the vessel, but had taken it back to the Downs with the aid of a mere boy, was considered one of the pluckiest episodes of those stirring times.

"INGSA'S" FRUITLESS RIDE

It was in the press-gang times. Two lads, serving at the farm of Houseby, in Beaquoyside, Birsay, had got astride their farm horses and were riding for Dounby in hot haste. This was the reason why: Two constables, George Mowat of Overbist, and "Ingsa," from Above-the-Hill, were in pursuit. As they passed the farm of Nistaben, in Knarston, Harray, "Ingsa" seized a horse which was quietly grazing on the fields. This he could do without let or hindrance, of course, being on the "King's errand," which also, as it happened at that time, "required haste." This horse was named Luggie. "Ingsa" mounted Luggie and led off in pursuit of the two mounted fugitives. He was closely followed by Geordie Mowat, who was clad in a "flitterie coat." This is not a coat of some specific style or fashion. A "flitterie coat" is a garment which has seen better days, for such experiences have coats in common with their wearers, and have also abundantly developed those "beautiful fringes" which are said to begin to show at the foot of a young man's trousers directly he begins to think himself a genius. Well, Geordie Mowat was dressed in a coat of this sort, and, notwithstanding the errand he was on, he carried a kind heart underneath and, truth to tell, had little love of the job on which he was now perforce engaged. When they arrived at the slap of Whickroo, "Ingsa," mounted on Luggie, was pressing hard behind the two youths, with Geordie Mowat "dalderin' an' rinnin'" in his flitterie coat, some short distance behind. Christina Scott, who observed the chase from Whickroo, got outside her cottage before the John Gilpin procession came up, and pulled out the wooden bars from across the slap through which they must pass. The two lads made the passage all right, but Christina then hastily replaced the bars before "Ingsa" came up, thus "pittin' a pin afore his neb." Her work done, she stood to await the upshot. "Pull oot the brods an' stand back," shouted "Ingsa" as he came up. "I'm not hurting you," he added; and indeed he could not, in his line, her guidman being at sea at the time. "If you're not injuring me you're injuring somebody else—I won't stand back," Christina answered. She did not know that Luggie was "skirry" or she would have flung her "bootie" to have scared him. (A "bootie" is a female Orcadian headpiece of the olden time.) Or perhaps she might have struck him with any weapon that came to hand, as some women in Stromness or Sandwick did with their "ware-picks" when the press-gang attempted to seize their male friends, for the soldier's blood in her was up. But she "let be for let be," so "Ingsa's" blood was not spilt at the slap o' Whickroo, as might have been. She merely stood passive, and he had to come down from "Luggie's" back and "rin the boards" back himself, which having been done, he mounted again and made off after his prey, followed as before. As they passed along, old Andrew of Curcabreck, who was standing outside, hailed them with, "This is bad work, Geordie!" "Bad wark, indeed, Andro!" replied Geordie, and off he went after "Ingsa." But they lost the day by their delay at the slap. The lads rode at speed through Tenston, and, leaving their horses, they took the road past the Stones of Stenness, away by Brodgar and then afoot to the Stenness hill, where they took to hiding. "Ingsa" had to turn back, as also Geordie Mowat, and "Luggie" of course. Indeed, neither "Luggie" nor Geordie seem to have had their heart in the work, and so they went about it as those who do have an unpleasant duty to perform, and they had to withstand a good deal of banter on the part of the rejoicing inhabitants.

A NEUK BED

Mansie o' Wheenalonga and James Isbister used to hide in the growing oats at Whilkow to escape the clutches of the press-gang. Indeed, this same James Isbister had to hide himself so often in the fields that he was dead tired of it at last, and said he should have one night under his own roof though they should come and take him. He was not, however, to get undisturbed rest, for Andrew of Curcabreck's wife came and "picked" on the flagstone roof of his "neuk-bed," and warned him to get up and decamp, for the constables were out again. So he had to fly to the fields once more. Do you know what a "neuk-bed" is, indeed? It is built of stone into the wall of the house, to which it forms a short wing or projection on the outside. These beds were very common in Orkney in the olden time. A relative of our informant's, who lives not very far from the scene of these tales, tells of a bed of this sort in which he lay when a young man. He describes how the bees had made a nest in the wall in summer-time, and how, in their ceaseless labours, they would come buzzing about the wall at all hours singing him to sleep. He might have truly quoted the lines of the great dramatist—

"And hushed with buzzing night-flies to his slumbers."

CAPTURED IN BED

There was a Spence lad who lived with his stepmother in the house of Gorn, in Harray, who was captured in bed in press-gang times. At that period it was customary to sleep "mither naked," and this youth was captured in this state. He commenced to put on his "harn sark" when he saw what was in the wind, but his stepmother gave him a linen shirt of the guidman's instead. He was now arrayed in his "snow-white seventeen-hunder linen," and to prepare him for his journey— his long journey as it proved to be, for he never came back— his step-mother gave him what was then considered a treat, "a bannock clined wi' butter." He, according to the account which has been handed down by tradition, ate the food very deliberately; it was his last meal in his native home, and no doubt had a peculiar relish for him. It may not be amiss here to say that the "harn sark" was made of coarsely-spun "hards" or tow. Anyone who has seen the old Orkney spinning-wheel may have also noticed a hole in the body thereof hard by the "headgear." This was the hole in which the "rock" was struck in tow-spinning. A common "emolument" in Orkney in the olden time was a "harn sark" and a shilling for a lassie to help "lay down the voar."

"Catch Him Noo, if Ye Can"

A youth was once beset by the press-gang at the farm of Midhouse, in Corrigall, Harray, but he escaped from the building by a back way, unseen by his pursuers. An old woman who was about saw him, however, and being constitutionally eloquent, and, like some of her sex, given to speaking in season and out of it, said to his would-be captors "Ha! Catch him noo, if ye can!" But they, like Burns, took her words as "a feckless maitter tae gae ane fash." They, in short, believed she was jesting. So the young man took to the hills, and was safe for that time. The truth is, he managed to dodge the press-gang till the war ended and there was no use for him as a soldier or a sailor.

Oh, Tammie Scott!

There was a lad named Thomas Firth, belonging to Mirbister, Harray, who was hunted by the press-gang. He took to the hills, and hid in a hollow or bank somewhere in or near "The Dees o' Beck," a muirland vale between Mirbister and the hillside of Birsay. Thomas Scott was among his pursuers. Scott, however, like he of the "flitterie coat," seems to have had little relish for such work, but, willy-nilly, he had no choice, but must needs do it when called upon, being a king's tenant, *i.e.*, a holder of Crown lands. In searching the moor for Firth, Scott, who was a little bit apart from the rest, on looking down into the crevices of a heather-clad bank, saw the youth for whom he was in quest in hiding beneath him. Firth also saw his pursuer, and, looking up in his face, said, "Oh Tammie Scott!" But Tammie Scott had a "fainfu' hert," and instead of seizing his lawful prey and delivering him up to his enemies, who were just approaching, waved his hand to the lad to be silent and lie close where he was, at the same time giving a loud cough to drown Firth's exclamation. So the youth was saved from going to the war at that time, though he may possibly have been taken afterwards. He escaped through his neighbour Tammie Scott's good heart and good cough, more than by his own cunning.

KATE HUNTLY AND THE PRESS-GANG

In the peat-moss of Sandwick, situated among the Birsay hills, there is a green spot on the south bank of a burn or water-course locally known as "Kit Huntlin's." This place was once the site of a human dwelling or "dellow." The walls, or the remains of the walls, of the house and "yards" are distinctly visible at the present day. Access to the water of the burn was conveniently obtained by a flight of stone steps from the water up the face of a steep incline to the level of the surrounding peat-moss.

A man cutting peats in the vicinity, some years ago "fasted" his horse on this green spot with a piece of rope tied to an iron stake, in hauling up which, a portion of turned wood was brought to the surface, of very elaborate workmanship, which had apparently been at one time part of a spinning wheel.

Tradition says that this place, or "dellow," was built and inhabited by a woman called Kate Huntly, and her son. During her husband's lifetime they had lived at a farm in the Hillside of Birsay, called the "Mill-gue," or the Millburn—a "gue" meaning a deep burn or watercourse.

The press-gang got information that there was a strapping young fellow at Mill-gue, the only son of his mother, and she was a widow. The person who gave this information was a neighbour, who dwelt in the same township in a house then called Rantan. The press-gang called at the house, but this young man was luckily not at home. Kate Huntly now saw that her boy was no longer safe in such a dangerous neighbourhood. Acting with decision, mother and son set to work and built a small house on the edge of this burn, choosing rather to be

> Birds of the wilderness,
> Blithesome and cumberless,

than live in a place where they were never sure of each other's company for a single hour. When the little house was finished, Kate and her son, having sold the ud-house at Mill-gue, removed to their eyrie in the bleak peat-moss. Kate's son strained every nerve to gather comforts to this retreat. He went to the Evie and Rendall shores for fish and ebb-meat; he gathered the "saave" of the heather and made ale; a few "bussy-broos" (native sheep) kept mother and son in clothing. The mother in the "hairst" went out on, or for "mullyow corn." These mullyows were old women or boys who were set as watchers, in the time of the run-rig, to see that one farmer did not make or take bands out of his neighbour's rig, or cut up all the fur-corn in the time of harvest. These mullyows, or little watchers, got the gleanings, the widow and the fatherless always being employed in this, the same as Ruth under the rules laid down for the Jewish harvest by the All-father. There were at the time wild animals called "kunnings." These "kunnings" and also the meat of the "bussy-broos" were "kitchen" for the "dellow-dwellers" or crofters. Thus lived Kate Huntly and her boy for a few years, happy in each other's society. But the envious, scheming "meal-payer" of Rantan was busy plotting how to bring misery into this lonely yet happy home. The King was always calling for more men to fight his battles, consequently the press-gang were scouring the country late and early, Sabbath day and week day, in quest of the best men. "Rantan" guided the press-gang how to act to secure Kate Huntly's boy. One fine day in the first of winter they stealthily approached this humble cot. But Kate, ever on the alert, had seen them or heard of their approach, and boldly met them herself at the junction of the Kit Huntly burn with the burn from the Twin of Rusht. She then and there denounced, with a widow's "malison," the farmer of Rantan. The officers and men accompanied Kate to her dwelling, where she regaled them with plenty of heather-ale. Her son, she told them, was away through the hill seeking (quarean) "kinings," and if they pleased to stop until he came home, he would go with them. And so

> The time wore on wi' sangs and clatter,
> An' aye the ale was growin' better.

After a while of drinking and singing, the men began to quarrel. Not. having room to "strike square from the shoulder" in the little house, the drunken combatants went outside to finish the strife. Meanwhile, Kate and her son, at a safe distance, were quietly looking on, she supplying a droughty combatant now and again with the fermented juice of the heather "saave." The members of the press-gang fought until they were almost naked, having torn the clothing off each other. After a sleep among the heather, they betook themselves to Kirkwall, and, being fertile in making excuses, they gave in as a reason of their nudity that Kate Huntly had torn the clothes of their backs defending her son. Poor Kate was now arraigned at Kirkwall to give an account of how she "rave" the "claes" off all the press-gang. Arrayed in a linsey-woolsey gown (this material was made of fine native-grown lint, and wool of the "bussy-broos," and was locally known as "nits and lice"), on her head and "shuthers" was a "scoorin' bootie," on her feet and legs were "ceutows" fastened down to the big toe of each foot with a "sprettow" of leather. Being placed at the "green table," she gave an account of the "riving" of the soldiers' clothes—in the Norse and Celtic mostly, as it has been handed down to us. "Stoon fa me, they set tew at alow tut-mut, efteran thei gaed tae a heich cullya shearg, at a hun's bark thei ware at a heigh cullya whumlie." All these words were used daily amongst old people in Orkney at the time of publication of the first edition in 1893; but for the sake of the present generation we may give the following translation:— "My averment on oath is, they (the press-gang) began to dispute and mutter among themselves, afterwards they began to talk louder and sharper, and in a dog's bark they were throwing one another down, and tumbling one another over very sharply." Kate Huntly was not found guilty of any misdemeanour towards His Majesty's officers.

The excitement of this trial likely told on the poor woman's frame, for in a very short time after she died, leaving her son alone to battle life's rough way. Her corpse was borne on "brod and blanket" to Birsay churchyard and buried in the south-west corner thereof, beside her husband.

Kate Huntly's boy, now being deprived of his mother's watchful care, and also being stealthily watched by the farmer of Rantan (the minion of the press-gang), was at length captured. He had dug a hole in the ground a little below the house, and covered it over with heather divots, in which to lie all night. There is an indentation below the ruins that is probably the site of this hiding-hole. He was surprised one morning taking his breakfast of heather ale and bere bannocks, was torn away from his home, and was ultimately killed in one of the many conflicts which the British had with the French.

Writing on this subject, in 1893, a correspondent says: The story, as well as its locality, has a special fascination, at least for me; and it may be of interest to your readers who care for such things to know that the stone stairs referred to in the tale still remain, though I would not take the responsibility of declaring that these are the identical steps built by Kate Huntly. All I can say is that they have been there since I remember. As of Barnes' "Stone Stairs,"

> Those rough stone stairs that stand so true
> With tread on tread, a foot-breadth wide,
> Have always climbed the sloping side
>   Of that steep ledge for me and you;
> But who can tell what pairs
> Of feet first trod these rough stone stairs?

Indeed the present steps may likely enough be the work of some herd-boy with a specially developed hump of "constructiveness," though, if so, who may deny that he was but "haarman' efter" the primary idea and work of Kate Huntly? Anyway, it would have been a very convenient appendage to her dwelling, as such a flight of stairs would have been passing useful in getting up and down from the hut above to the water, some twenty feet below. According to one version of the tradition, her real name was not Huntly, but Corrigal, the name Huntly being probably derived from the persecutions to which she was subjected. Also, that while the men—Harray men—were sitting in her dwelling regaling themselves with the heather ale, she slipped outside, and Samson-like, pulled out the "maintree" of the hut, thus burying them in the ruins, ending the tragedy, not at the "green table" in Kirkwall, nor on the far-off field of battle, but summarily, and on the spot. But the different versions of the traditional legend, as well as other evidence, almost certainly place the date of Kate Huntly's dwelling in her hut in the far moorland much farther back than the beginning of the eighteenth century, so that if a press-gang legend at all, it must belong to the time of the Marlborough wars with the French. The word "queen" should, therefore, have been used instead of "king" in the published version. By the way, as we have begun to criticise, in a friendly fashion, should not she have had her "sprettows" fastened to the toe *next* her big toe, according to use and wont in the olden time. But these are small matters. There is a house named Rantan in the district where Kate Huntly lived prior to her removing to her desert eyrie, but whether this was named after a former house of that name is not known. Curiously enough, the present house of Rantan was built by a woman much in the same way in which Kate Huntly built her house, with this difference, that Annie Johnston, the builder of the later dwelling, had no son to lend her a helping hand. Nevertheless, it was marvellous how, with her single pair of hands, she made herself a dwelling on the edge of the wilderness. I knew this old woman well. She was a woman of "infinite jest," and I remember her holding many a discourse on "Religion and Morals" of which Presbytery or Assembly never received a "report." How she would have scorned youthful ignorance on such important points as the "Burgher" and "Anti-Burgher" controversy, I remember yet. Many a woman has been immortalised in story who had not a tithe of the claim that "Annie o' Rantan" had. But of the old house of Rantan, if such there ever was, there is no trace, nor breath of tradition, to point to its site. Mill-gue, where, according to the published version of the tradition, Kate Huntly's persecutor lived is, however, a dwelling still. According to the records kept in Edinburgh, a man named Thomas Spence was living in Mill-gue in the year 1736. And, according to a local tradition, that house was first built and inhabited by a William Spence, who came from Evie, and had to take his "kindling fire" with him in an iron pot, so much were his new neighbours against his coming amongst them. So he might have been the husband of Kate Huntly in the times of the wars of Queen Anne, or, allowing a large margin for tradition mixing up her characters, he might possibly have been the Rantan of this tale. The whole is hoary and shadowy. In these days, when the tourist penetrates to almost every nook and corner, it is not a little strange that the "savage waste" where this legend of Kate Huntly has its location and its name, is as yet an undiscovered country to whose bourne no traveller comes. No ginger-beer bottle may there be seen as a memento of his visit. Yet nowhere in the islands can there be seen a richer bloom on the heather, or wilder scenery, or nicer views. To the dweller in the Orcadian, or any other metropolis, there could not be shown a better place for learning the falsehood of Charles Lamb's doctrine of "the sweet security of streets." And from the summit of the "Twin of Rusht," referred to in the tale, may be seen no less than seven churches dedicated to the Orcadian St. Magnus, chief among these being his old red sandstone shrine in famous Kirkwall town. From such a vantage ground may also be observed, as indicated, quite other than physical sights and "views"—views far-reaching—showing how essentially and primarily anthropomorphic the universe is: how, in the meanest, as in the greatest—in Kate Huntly no less than in Magnus the Holy—there is a glory and a mysticism oftimes in humanity; and across the wastes of Time can thence be seen how "Souls burn for souls, spirits to spirits cry."

RESCUED BY A FEMALE

The press-gang, in trying to get men from the islands of Graemsay and Pharay, had numerous difficulties to cope with. Not the least of these was the strong tides. When they were seen approaching Graemsay, the young men would take a boat and pull out in the eddies of the tide. The press-gang, not being "to the manner born," in a great many cases could not get at them. One day the press-gang stealthily approached

Graemsay in such a way that the inhabitants did not see them until they had landed. Being harvest time, the people were all busy cutting the corn, with no thought of the approaching danger. On the alarm being given, the male portion of the population at once made off for the noust of Vaevil, and had just time to get into a boat. Before they could put off from the shore, however, one of the swiftest of the press-gang had his hands on the boat's gunwale. The Graemsay young women had accompanied their sweethearts to the noust, and had helped to shove down the boat. One heroine, seeing a soldier seizing the boat's gunwale, laid hold of the broken "nave" of an oar and dealt such a well directed, powerful stroke, that the hand had to be amputated. The boatmen shoved off the boat, and before the press-gang got round their boat to Vaevil, the Graemsay lads were sitting in the roost of Milbunas. The heroic young woman referred to above, Sinclair to name, was a daughter of the house of Deean. The "nave" of the oar was kept in Graemsay Church for a great many years. Inadvertently, however, it was thrown out and lost the year before the lighthouses were built on Graemsay. A year later, schism entered the island, and the superstitious believe this was the natural result of the "nave" being lost.

WHIPPED THROUGH THE FLEET

George Sutherland, one of those impressed for Tankerness, was said to be case-grown. He was very strong. Once he deserted, was caught and was whipped through the fleet. When he came to his own ship a chair was put down to the boat to haul him on board. Slinging the chair aside, he seized a rope and in true sailor style clambered on board. When he reached the deck he challenged any one of the crew to try him with the knuckles. No one dared to accept the challenge. The captain, a Highlander, said, "He's a grand fellow, doctor. Take him and give him a glass of grog, and dress his back carefully. If I had known he was such a good fellow I would not have had him whipped." After the war George came back to Tankerness and married. Hearing that a vain fellow had been boasting that he was the strongest man at the north side of the burn of Stenswick, George at the next Toab market went up to the bully and asked him if he had said so, and was answered in the affirmative. "Do you think so yet?" "I do." "Put your hand in mine to that effect." "Oh! oh! oh! Give me back my hand," yelled the bully, for the blood was squirting from his finger tips. George relaxed his hold and said, "Do you still think you are the strongest man in Tankerness?" "No, you are stronger than I am." Pleased with this feat of strength, George turned away with his friend, saying, "I could have made his hand as dry as a mummy's if I had chosen to have done so." This little speech reminded the bystanders of his doughty deeds in Egypt, when he was there with the British Fleet during those stirring times.

THE EUNSONS OF MIDHOUSE

William Eunson, Andrew Eunson, and James Eunson of Midhouse, Deerness, were often hunted by the press-gang. One time, William was passing through the hole in the Horn of Halley, when the heel of his shoe got caught among the rocks. Giving a desperate wrench, the shoe gave way and he got free. Andrew and James were visiting their aunt in Windbreck on another occasion, when the hated press-gang were seen approaching. A nook in the wall, concealed by a press, was their only chance of escape. Into this they both got, and the press was at once replaced; but the hiding-place having only been made for one, the press had to be kept a little further from the wall than usual. One of the officers noticed that the press was too far from the wall and asked the reason. He was told that a wall flag prevented it getting farther back. One of the press-gang, more curious than the others, pushed his staff into the recess and actually touched the head of one of the hiding men, but thought the obstacle was the wall. It was an anxious time for Jane Stove when she beheld the staff passed over the press where her step-mother's nephews were—Andrew being her lover. After these troublesome times were over, there was a marriage at Windbreck.

A DOCTOR'S PROMISE

M agnus Gaudie and his sweetheart, Jane Linklater, were servants to George Delday in Halley, during press-gang times. Gaudie was without friends among the press-gang, so he had to be wary. The shores near Halley are well provided with caves suitable for hiding-places. The cave and castle of the Repenting Stool were the chief resort of those in Kirbuster who fled from the press-gang. It is a cave of peculiar form and can be entered from above or below. Yet two men in it could defy a thousand. Descending from above over a steep slope, you come to a hole a few feet in diameter, almost perpendicular, with rock and clay forming its sides. From the side of this hole an opening passes to another outlet in the floor of this cave, and the roof of another. On the rocky platform between these holes fugitives often rested. A ledge forming a seat was a little comfort to the weary, hunted men hiding there. In the cave Gaudie found three men from Midhouse, one from Horrie, and some others. Food was lowered down to them from above, or placed in the lower cave by a boat, and they lay there for weeks. It being bere seed time, they were sadly missed at home, and it seemed as if the seed could not be got in the ground in time. Dr Groat, navy doctor for Orkney, was proprietor of Halley, and came on a visit to see the farm, when Gaudie was in hiding. He saw Delday sweating at the sowing, ploughing and harrowing. Asking Delday why he was so busy, he was answered that no man could be got for love or money until the press-gang ceased their attentions. "Get your servant man to come and work, and I will certify that he is unfit for service," was Dr Groat's rejoinder. Trusting in this promise, Gaudie was brought home. Soon after this the press-gang put in their appearance. Jane Linklater was prepared to receive them warmly. Suspecting their approach one night, she put on the muckle pot, and when they came she stood with the big ladle in her hand and dared anyone to enter. For a long time she kept them at bay, and then Delday, believing in the doctor's promise, bade her let them enter. Soon after, Gaudie was on the road to the town, and Delday on horseback going to remind the doctor of his promise. The doctor wanted to let the man be sent away, but Delday, unlike some tenants, was not afraid to speak his mind plainly to the laird. On this occasion he had to speak sharply ere he gained the exemption of Gaudie. When Gaudie was presented to the doctor for examination, Dr Groat said, "Where are your sons that you bring such a man as that to me?" This was too much for John Foubister's temper, and he replied, "When we bring you men, you will not keep them, so we'll bring no more." "Hold your tongue or I will send you aboard of the tender yourself, for you are fit for the service," testily answered the doctor. Soon after these adventures Gaudie was married to his faithful Jeannie.

A TARTAR

John Irvine, an old man-o'-war's man, lived at the Ness, near to the town of Stromness, and, like a retired sailor, often went into the town to have a glass with an old crony. One day when he was sipping his grog, word was brought to him that a lieutenant and boat's crew had landed from a warship and were impressing his servant man. Running to the shore, he saw the boat leaving the beach as he came to the top of the banks. Seeing he had no time to lose, he leaped over the banks, rushed into the water and grasped the boat. He was up to the waist in water, but he dragged the boat back, threw the officer and his crew out, and took his man ashore. He then turned to the officer and told him of the battles he had fought, the ships he had boarded, and defied him and his crew to take his man from him, old as he was. Having seen his agility, felt the grip of his hand and the strength of his arm, the bedraggled officer left him master of the field. Irvine used to tell how he killed a bully on board a man-of-war. One day the captain of the ship on which Irvine was sailing was visiting another captain aboard his ship and there he saw that one of the men was ill-using the others, knocking them down and kicking them, for no offence, but merely to gratify a morbid sense of humour. Irvine's captain remonstrated with the other for allowing his men to be so brutally used. "O, that is nothing. That is a splendid fellow. There is not a man in either of our ships that can say anything to that man." This led to a dispute between the two captains, when at last Irvine's captain accepted a bet of one hundred guineas that he would get a match for the bully. Irvine was sent for, and as soon as he stepped over the stranger ship, the bully rushed at him and tried to knock him through the gangway. Irvine coolly pushed him aside, and, when he was passing, struck him a blow on the side and lifted him to the taffrail, where he lay a few minutes, and was lifted down dead.

MAD HARRY

In the district of Ireland, near Stromness, in the time of the press-gang, there lived a young man named Harry Clouston, commonly known as Mad Harry. He had been at Davis Straits, and was now a fisherman. One of the trophies he had taken home from his ship was a blubber knife, with which he used to defy the press-gang when they attempted to take him, which often occurred. It is even said that he habitually took the blubber knife to bed with him, so as to be ready for an emergency. One night he dreamed that the press-gang were coming in to seize him, and, when only half awake, he made a grab for the blubber knife and cut himself severely with it. Another day his mother came and told him that the press-gang were approaching, and he set off for the hills, taking a gun along with him. Finding that some of his pursuers were apparently gaining on him, he took his stand on a certain knowe, and drawing a circle round it, he said that the first who tried to enter it would be a dead man. Considering discretion the better part of valour, none of the press-gang dared to approach within the prescribed limit which he had drawn, especially seeing that he held his gun ready to fire. This time he got clear. Shortly afterwards he bought a herring boat. One night his men did not come down, and he was very dissatisfied, as the other boats were getting herrings. Next day he swore he would have herrings if he should go to the end of the earth for them. Accordingly he did go out, but he never returned to land. The last that was heard of him was his cries as his boat was being wrecked on the sunken rocks of the Lother.

A DARING PROCEEDING

A man named James Matches, belonging to Holm, had a very exciting adventure in connection with the press-gang.

On one particular occasion he was coming home from Davis Straits, two other ships being in company with his one, and when almost within sight of land a boat left each of the vessels, in order to try and escape being captured.

A cutter, however, which had been lying in wait for the whalers, pursued the boats and the crews of the whole of them were captured.

The cutter made for the coast of Ireland. One day most of the watch had been called below for mess, and only a few men were left to look after the captives.

The hardy Straitsmen, who had been watching for something favourable to turn up, considered this was a splendid opportunity for trying to secure their liberty, and they succeeded, after an exciting struggle, in overpowering the watch and closing them down below. The ship was then steered into a bay and anchored.

The imprisoned commander of the cutter read to the mutineers an Act, showing them the enormity of the crime they had committed in seizing the vessel, but offered them all a free pardon if they would give up the ship and surrender.

Instead of complying with this request, however, the old whalers took the cutter's boats and went ashore. They then dispersed in twos and threes, and travelled all night, hiding in all sorts of out-of-the-way places during the day, till they arrived at a seaport, where they had a chance of getting a vessel to their own country.

But in the course of their long journey they were so sorely pressed by hunger that James Matches used to declare that he sold even the napkin he had round his neck for a common bannock.

Matches, after many hair-breadth escapes, eventually reached Orkney in safety, however, and for a considerable number of years afterwards resided in Holm.

He subsequently left that parish and removed to Deerness, where he remained for the rest of his days, highly respected. He died at a ripe old age and was much esteemed by his acquaintances.

Someone once asked him what would have happened to himself and his old whaling comrades if the enraged commander of the cutter had caught them after leaving the ship. He replied that every one of them would have been hanged to the yardarm like dogs.

DRAMATIC END TO A TYRANT

In bringing these press-gang stories to a close, it may be pointed out that the navy at the beginning of last century had an evil reputation, and was far from attractive to a peaceable people such as the Orcadians. The "cat" was at that time often in evidence, and it was almost a daily occurrence for some poor sailor to be lashed for a trifling offence.

Our closing sketch under this head shows that the victims of this tyranny sometimes turned upon their tormentors, preferring death to such brutality.

An old Sanday man who had been impressed, but who lived to return to his native island, used to tell a thrilling tale illustrative of the state of matters we have just described above.

On board the ship on which he was sent to serve, there was a petty officer of a tyrannous disposition, who made life a burden to the unfortunate sailors who were under his control, and he had a special spite to a big burly seaman, who was the life of the mess to which he belonged.

On one occasion, this mite of an officer reported that the sailor had used insulting language to him, and had the poor fellow court-martialled.

The upshot of the trial was that the sailor was condemned

to receive the usual number of lashes which were so lavishly administered at that time for such an offence—these to be applied by the boatswain's mate.

The vicious little officer, glorifying in the job, however, insisted that he should do the lashing himself. Not being nearly tall enough to administer the "cat" with effect from the deck, he got a small platform erected on which to stand.

When all was ready for the brutalising punishment to begin, the culprit was led out, stripped and ready to be fastened into position to receive the lashes.

The petty officer stood on the platform with a cruel leer on his face, brandishing the "cat."

The prisoner took in the whole cruel scene in one swift glance, and as his tormentor at that moment used some insulting epithet, he quickly resolved upon his course of action. Suddenly springing upon the platform, the sailor lifted the officer in his arms, and before the astonished crew grasped his object or could interfere, he sprang overboard with the little tyrant, shouting that he would make crab's meat of him.

The sailor preferred death to dishonour, and if the truth must be told, the crew of the vessel, whilst secretly rejoicing at getting rid of a petty tyrant, were saddened with the thought of parting with their ill-fated companion in such a terribly dramatic manner.

PART III—WITCH AND OTHER STORIES

WITCH AND OTHER STORIES

In the stories which follow, the chief characters are real, and the dates of trials and executions are those which appear in the official indictments. When we read of the crimes perpetrated by our forefathers upon innocent women in the name of religion, we are apt to become Pharisaical, and to feel thankful that, in this enlightened century, we have got rid of such superstitions. We have certainly got beyond the burning of witches, but have we not all more or less a little of the superstitious in our nature still? In Orkney, late last century, there were those who believed that the approaching death of a member of one of the leading county families was heralded by the wailing of the banshie.

The North Ronaldsay people tell of a young man who was going home late at night when he had a strange encounter with a white figure. Thinking at first that some of his companions were trying to frighten him, he chased the object. As he passed a certain house, it mysteriously disappeared. When he was rushing away from the building he heard peculiar shrieks, evidently above and behind him. A few days afterwards a death occurred at the house in question, and the people were convinced that the supposed apparition had been sent as a warning of the sad event. In the same island the house where fairies were last seen, surrounded by a flame, was pointed out, until the end of last century, and was known as the Blue Room.

At the north end of Shapinsay some people, when their cattle took ill, were inclined to blame an old woman for their misfortunes. They sometimes lost the "profit" of their milk, and the plan they adopted to get it back was to steal a trifling article, such as a turnip, from the person whom they suspected to have thrown a spell over themselves or their gear. This was considered an infallible remedy for preventing a continuance of such mischief. Amongst some people, the belief obtained that a sufferer from rheumatism who carried a potato on his person would get immediate and permanent relief.

THE WESTRAY STORM WITCH

M ost of the culprits tried for witchcraft in Orkney in the seventeenth century were old women. Janet Forsyth, known as the Storm Witch of Westray, was, however, an exception. When she was first accused of holding communication with the Evil One she was quite a young woman, about twenty years of age; and her biography, taken from the indictment upon which she was tried, reads more like fiction than a dry, musty, legal record of the actions of a felon. Janet, at the time our story commences, had a lover in the person of Benjamin Garrioch, a young farmer in the island of Westray. On both sides the love flame was as strong as it was sincere; and yet their courtship did not run quite smoothly. Janet Forsyth was as great an adept at pouting and flirting as are the more modern daughters of Eve. Sometimes, therefore, she encouraged her lover's attentions, and sent him home the happiest man in the parish; but quite as frequently she treated him with the most perfect indifference without any apparent reason.

One summer morning in the beginning of July, 1627, Garrioch and three companions when approaching the beach to go out for a sail, were met by Janet Forsyth, who pled with them not to put to sea that day. At first she would give no reason for her strange request, but, finding that the young men were inclined to treat her interference as a joke, she began to urge her objections with greater force and vehemence. She told them that she had had a dream the previous night, from which she was certain that if they went out in the boat that day some dreadful calamity would befall them. Her lover pointed to the sea, on which there was not a ripple, also to the heavens, which were cloudless, and, in the hope of dispelling what he considered her groundless fears, playfully told her there were no tokens of danger there. When the boat was launched, however, and Garrioch was about to spring into it, his sweetheart threw her arms round his neck and made one last passionate appeal in the short and simple sentence, "Oh, don't leave me, Ben!" Then, as if feeling ashamed at her own weakness, and without giving Ben time to make an answer, she ran up the bank and disappeared.

This demonstration on the part of his sweetheart momentarily upset Garrioch, for hitherto she had been coy, shy, and reserved rather than forward, impulsive, or demonstrative; but the blood of the old Norse Vikings coursed through his veins. The sea had an irresistible attraction for him, and so, putting the fears of his sweetheart down to a nervous whim, his little boat was soon gliding out towards the Westray Firth.

Boat and crew never returned. Fog, which is the hand-maiden of heat in those northern latitudes, speedily enveloped the island, so that Garrioch and his companions were apparently unable to find their way back again. Days, weeks, months, and years sped past, and the fate of the unfortunate men still remained a mystery.

It was at this period that Janet Forsyth first began to be suspected of witchcraft and sorcery. Her superstitious neighbours knew that she had foretold the disaster that was to befall Garrioch and his companions, and they concluded that she could only have got her information through intercourse with the Evil One.

Troubles, it has been said, rarely come singly, but follow each other in quick succession. This was the experience of Janet Forsyth, for a few months after the disappearance of her sweetheart, she lost her father, who was the only remaining relative she had on the island. From that time onward, she took no interest in anything transpiring around her. She became a victim to melancholia, and shunned the companionship of her neighbours. Indeed, for days together she never left her own house. There was no window in her humble dwelling, but venturesome boys who had climbed up on the thatched roof, and had peeped through the hole which did duty both as a chimney and for giving light to the lonely occupant, had reported that she sat with her arms folded, crooning a plaintive song—a circumstance which gave rise to the belief that this was her method of luring the Storm King from the caverns of the deep.

When a fresh breeze was blowing, and the angry billows came tumbling in upon the beach, she could often be seen hurrying down to a noust where her father had kept his boat, and she frequently put to sea when her hardy neighbours believed it impossible that her little craft could live. But she seemed to have a charmed life and returned to the island over and over again after she had been given up for lost. In this way she earned the title of the Storm Witch.

When fishermen went to sea and sustained any damage, either personally or to their gear, Janet Forsyth got the credit of the mishap. For instance, Robert Reid, a Westray fisherman, took ill one day when out in his boat, and on landing he accused the young woman of being a witch, alleging that she had thrown an evil spell over him. Janet Forsyth did not deign to give any answer to the charge, but she threw a bucket of salt water over her accuser, and he declared that he had been healed instantaneously by this simple means. It might have been though that Reid would have been satisfied with such an easy and rapid cure; but he was not, for he appeared as a witness against the Storm Witch when she was subsequently tried for sorcery at Kirkwall.

The people ultimately believed so strongly in her powers as a witch that, in times of sickness, they coaxed her to visit the sufferers; and, if the indictment is to be believed, she wrought wonderful cures amongst them. It might therefore have been thought that the Storm Witch would, in such circumstances, have earned the gratitude of those who consulted her; but it so happened that cattle and horses occasionally died, and the owners never hesitated to put down these losses to the credit of Janet Forsyth.

At last, matters reached a crisis. A large vessel was seen driving helplessly in upon the island, in midst of a terrific gale,

and the inhabitants felt perfectly certain that they were about
to have a rich harvest from the sea. The beach was crowded
with people, but no proposal was made to render assistance
to the crew of the apparently doomed ship. By and by, however,
the Storm Witch forced herself through the crowd of onlookers.
The woman knew well that an appeal for aid would have no
response; and so, casting a withering look of contempt at the

people, she proceeded to the beach, set sail on her little boat, and put off to the rescue alone.

The islanders stood aghast at the hardihood of the Storm Witch. It was believed nothing human could live in such a gale, even if the boat had been the best belonging to the island, which it was not. When the frail little craft was caught in the swirling tide which runs round Westray, it could be seen rising on the crest of a wave, and then it would disappear for such a length of time that it was surmised it had gone down. Once more, however, it would come in sight, always drawing nearer and nearer the vessel which was so rapidly drifting towards destruction.

At length the vessel was boarded. The peril in which the crew was placed evidently prevented them from commenting on their strange visitor. The Storm Witch hurried aft to the wheel, gave a few orders in quick succession which were promptly obeyed, and the vessel was speedily run into Pierowall Bay, where it was anchored in safety.

The sailors, who had given themselves up for lost, now crowded around the Storm Witch, offering her their thanks for their rescue, while the captain tried to persuade her to accept a well-filled purse in acknowledgment of her daring and timely services. But she firmly and resolutely declined the present. In fact, she refused to converse with the sailors further than to express the wish that somebody might, if opportunity occurred, do as much for her Ben.

Now the crew were safe, the Storm Witch left the vessel with as little ceremony as she had joined it, and a few hours later she was sitting plaintively singing at the peat-fire of her lonely home, as if all that she had done was simply a matter of course.

If this poor woman had lived in the twentieth century, her heroic action would have called forth the plaudits of the civilised world; but the superstitious generation to which she belonged could only see in her conduct fresh proof of her connection with the Evil One.

She was accordingly arrested on a charge of being a rank witch, and was tried in St Magnus Cathedral three weeks later.

A number of witnesses were examined, from whom the

prosecutor elicited the story of the alleged misdeeds of the Storm Witch, much in the same terms as we have given them.

The jury, after a short consultation, brought in a verdict of guilty against the prisoner. The judge asked if she had any reason to give why sentence of death should not be passed on her.

As the Storm Witch rose slowly to her feet, a solemn hush passed over the audience. "I am innocent," she said, "of the crime which has been laid to my charge. In saving the crew of the vessel referred to, I had no assistance but from God, with a powerful arm to guide the tiller of my boat and a quick eye to avoid the breakers which surrounded me. The remedies I employed to heal the sick were simple, and I believe imagination on the part of the patients played a very prominent part in restoring them to health. As to the horses and cattle which died, I assure you that so far as I know, death resulted from natural causes. But I have no desire to live, and the sentence which you are about to pass has no terrors for me."

The judge, having expressed his horror of the crime of witchcraft, of which she had been found guilty, said he had no alternative but to order that the next day she should be taken from prison with her hands tied behind her back, led to the Gallows Ha', where she was to be fastened to a stake, to be worried to death by the hangman, and her body thereafter to be burnt to ashes.

Whilst the sentence was being delivered, a number of naval sailors entered the Court, and, though they knew nothing of the merits of the case, applauded the sentence as heartily as the rest of the audience.

When the noise had subsided, the prisoner turned round and faced the people with a contemptuous smile on her face, but as her gaze fell on one of the strange sailors, all her fortitude seemed to desert her, and she fell to the floor with an agonised scream on her lips of "Save me, Ben; save me!"

In a moment the sailor was beside her, and raising her in his arms began calling her all sorts of endearing names.

The whole thing had occurred so suddenly that Judge and officers were for the time completely taken by surprise. When the Sheriff-Depute recovered from the shock, however, he sternly ordered the sailor to give the prisoner over to the charge of the officers of the Court, and intimated that he only refrained from punishing him as his conduct deserved, on the ground that he had just returned from fighting the King's enemies in France.

Thereafter the poor woman was led to the condemned cell, making the aisle of the Cathedral loudly echo with her heart-piercing screams.

The night on which the Storm Witch was condemned was a memorable one in the history of Kirkwall. The British Fleet, under the command of the Duke of Buckingham, had been driven on the Orkney coast by stress of weather, and had taken refuge in Kirkwall Bay. In the early part of the day, the officers had been entertained to a cake and wine banquet, and in the evening, the municipal rulers, with many of the county gentry, enjoyed the hospitality of the Admiral on the Flagship. As was usual on these occasions, the town's officers came in for a large share of the drink which had been left over at the banquet, whilst the populace had several barrels of ale served out to them at the Market Cross.

In these circumstances, the hangman and his two companions who had been appointed to remain in the cell beside the condemned woman during the night also went in for a tremendous carousal.

At ten o'clock the following morning, a large crowd had assembled in Broad Street, Kirkwall, to see the poor woman led to her doom, amongst these being a number of the officers and men of the fleet. The Cathedral bell began to toll, and all anxiously awaited the prisoner to emerge from the cell.

After a short pause, the Sheriff-Depute and Provost Craigie proceeded to the cell to ascertain the cause of delay, but hastily returned, reporting that they had found the door unlocked, the hangman and his assistants asleep, and the prisoner gone.

Messengers were at once dispatched in all directions with orders to prevent the escape of the Storm Witch, whilst a thorough search of the town was made, in the hope that she might be captured there.

A few years afterwards, Bailie Baikie of Kirkwall, when passing through Manchester on his way to London, was much surprised to find a merchant there having on his signboard such an unmistakable Orcadian name as "Benjamin Garrioch," and he entered the shop to see the individual. To his surprise he found the Storm Witch of Westray in charge. But how changed she was. She was no longer the tired-out, grief-stricken woman she appeared to be when on her trial in Kirkwall, but was full of life and vivacity, and she was at least ten years younger looking.

The Bailie having given an undertaking that he would keep the secret of the happy couple, they freely told him their story. It appeared that when Garrioch and his three companions left Westray they were caught in the fog, they had been picked up by a man-of-war vessel, in which they had been carried off to take part in the war, which was then being waged with France. Garrioch was in one of the war vessels anchored in Kirkwall Bay on the day his sweetheart was being tried for witchcraft, but when he entered the court he had not the slightest suspicion that he should see Janet Forsyth in such a cruel situation. It was only when she turned round to face the audience that he made the discovery, and from that moment, he formed the resolve that he should effect her escape. Knowing that the hangman and his assistants were addicted to drink, he had no difficulty in getting a supply conveyed to them, and with it he succeeded in giving each of them a strong sleeping draught. Watching his opportunity, which was easily got owing to the entertainment of the municipal rulers on the flagship, he got into the condemned cell, and lost no time in releasing his sweetheart. The vessel which she had saved from destruction a few weeks previously at Westray was then lying in Inganess Bay ready to put to sea, and the captain gladly assisted in the rescue of the Storm Witch.

Janet Forsyth was by this means conveyed to Liverpool, where she resided with the captain's wife till Garrioch, a week or two later, arrived at Portsmouth with the fleet, when he took French leave of the services of Charles I.

Garrioch and his wife never again ventured back to Orkney. They were most successful in business in their new home, however, and there are to be found in Manchester at the present day, descendants of the Westray Storm Witch.

THE SPITTING WITCH

All the Orkney witches had some distinguishing peculiarity of their own. Janet Rendal of Rigga, in the parish of Rendall, who was a witch of some repute at the beginning of the seventeenth century, seems to have adopted, at least in the early part of her career, the habit of spitting over her left shoulder when she wished specially to mystify her neighbours, and so earned for herself the sobriquet of the Spitting Witch.

The cot of Rigga was well adapted for the character which its occupant had assumed. It consisted of one apartment, which served as hen-house, pighouse, bedroom, and kitchen combined, and even in the daytime the place was always wrapped in gloom. The walls of the house were built of stones and turf, the roof being covered with flags, overlaid with moss and straw. The inside of the building was void of plaster, but was thickly coated with soot; and the peat fire which occupied the centre of the clay floor kept the apartment filled with smoke, because the only outlets for it were the many chinks in the walls, or through a hole in the roof.

One dark, stormy night in the winter of 1609, a knock came to the door of Rigga. Janet Rendal, without as much as turning her head, shouted, "Come in, Jean Matches, I've been expecting you."

The visitor slowly opened the door, as if she were afraid to cross the threshold.

"Dinna stand there wi' your leg drawn up under ye like a hen on a rainy day, woman. Shut the door an' come ben to the fire. Ye needna' stan' glowering there as if I intended to eat ye."

These words were uttered in a series of gasps and at the end of each clause Janet Rendal spat over her left shoulder, as if to emphasise what she was saying.

Jean Matches, accepting of this snappish invitation, crept up to the fire, and having got a seat on a box, sat gazing into the face of the Spitting Witch, without uttering a word. And no wonder. The Spitting Witch did look uncanny. Her black eyes sparkled and gleamed in the flickering light of the half-burnt peats, and her complexion, more jaundiced than swarthy, assumed a most sickly hue.

After a long pause, the Spitting Witch broke the silence. "Ye hae come, dootless, to consult me aboot yer husband. Ye want to ken whaur he is, an' what he is doing. If I tell ye a' this, mair than likely ye'll gang awa' an' denounce me to the minister as a witch."

"Na, na," was the reply of the visitor, "I'll ne'er lift my tongue against ye. But how did ye ken it was me that was at the door whenever I knocked, and also what my message was before I had spoken?"

"If I were to answer ye, my woman, ye wadna believe my statement, sae we'll say nae mair on that point. Let us to the business on hand."

"Weel, can ye tell me onything o' my husband?" earnestly asked the visitor.

The witch, without answering, rose from her seat and proceeded to a wooden press which stood in a recess at the opposite side of the fire. Taking a small basin therefrom, she filled it with water and threw a piece of burning peat in the centre of it. Holding the vessel at arm's length, she mumbled a few meaningless words, and then spat thrice over her left shoulder. Having repeated this ceremony three times, she resumed her seat. Speaking in a sort of dreamy way, she began to address her visitor: "Your husband is in a distant land, and amongst strangers. He has been very ill, but he is getting better noo, and will soon be hame again."

"Oh, thank ye, Janet, for the relief ye hae gi'en me. I was sair annoyed at the lang absence o' Andrew, but ye hae set my fears at rest, an' I'll gang hame the nicht wi' an easier mind than I hae had for mony months."

Producing a small cheese, she put it in the hands of the Spitting Witch, and then proceeded to the door, her whole demeanour showing that she was afraid to remain longer in such an uncanny place.

The Spitting Witch, having got rid of her visitor, gave vent to her feelings by addressing her collie dog, which was lying dozing as close up to the fire as he could get: "Poor Help. Ye hae mair gumption in ye than thae foolish folks that come to me for information. That puir creature got the news aboot her husband frae ane o' the sailors wha was on the ship wi' him, just as I got it mysel', and yet she wadna believe it till it was confirmed by a witch. Oh, the stupidity o' the human race."

Such visits as the one just described were of common occurrence. Janet Rendal's neighbours were anxious to know what was going to happen in advance, especially if good fortune was promised; and the Spitting Witch, who much needed the assistance she got for the information she imparted, rarely sent any of them home with a sore heart. Notwithstanding this, she was by no means a favourite. She lived very much apart from the other residenters in the parish, and when sickness or death came amongst them or their stock, the Spitting Witch was, as a rule, blamed for being the cause of these misfortunes. If the children were noisy or disobedient, mothers would terrify them by merely mentioning the name of the Spitting Witch.

Janet Rendal was thus suspected by her neighbours and feared by their children. But there was one exception. Between the family of Gilbert Sandie of Isbister and Janet Rendal's friends there had been a feud for generations. The laird of Isbister therefore lost no opportunity of harassing the Spitting Witch, and frequently reported her to the Rendall Session for sorcery. Strangely enough, however, the laird's only son, a child seven years of age, had contracted a warm friendship with the Spitting Witch. Whenever he got the chance, he slipped off to Rigga, and would be there for hours at a time. Threats, thrashings, and punishments of all kinds had been tried for the purpose of making the little fellow give up his strange fancy for the old woman, but without avail.

At length the boy took ill, and his one cry was to see Granny Rendal, the Spitting Witch. The laird of Isbister was a man of means and he spared no expense in providing toys and all sorts of nick-nacks for his dying child; but these were thrown aside as soon as received, without giving any satisfaction or pleasure.

Gilbert Sandie was an unhappy man. He was tossed hither and thither between parental affection and pride. His son was evidently dying, and his heart was set upon seeing the Spitting Witch. But how could his father, an elder in he kirk, invite a character like Janet Rendal to his house, especially when he remembered that his own and her forebears were deadly foes?

As the child grew more persistent in his pleadings to see the old woman, however, and refused to be comforted whilst this wish remained unsatisfied, Gilbert Sandie began to ask himself what she had ever done to him that he should keep up the old family quarrel; and he felt rather uneasy in mind when he recalled the fact that hitherto all the persecution had been on his part.

The upshot of these communings was that he went off to Rigga, and no sooner had he told Janet Rendal of the illness of his child, and of his desire to see her, than the old woman volunteered to accompany him back to Isbister.

The moment she entered the house the child gave a joyous scream of welcome. "Oh, granny," he exclaimed, "I thought you were never coming to see me."

It was with wet eyes that the old woman bent over the child to kiss him, for her experienced eye told her that the little fellow had not long to live.

"Why do you greet, granny?" asked the child. "When I used to go down to Rigga you were always funny and made me happy. Granny, tell Help to be an old woman."

In a twinkling, the old woman's dog was sitting on its hind legs, had on its owner's mutch and spectacles, and looked a demure old wife. The child was so delighted with the ludicrous appearance of the dog that he seemed all at once to forget his trouble, and laughed and clapped his hands in boisterous glee. At the child's request the dog went through a number of tricks, such as it had been in the habit of performing when he used to visit Rigga before he took ill. The child then asked to get a ride from Help.

When the dog saw the little patient being lifted out of the bed, it seemed to understand instinctively what was expected of it, and began to gambol joyously round the room.

The fond father, who had been a happy spectator of all that was going on, was delighted at the apparent improvement that had so rapidly taken place in the condition of his child, and was no doubt picturing to himself the time when he would be running about strong and healthy as ever.

But he was soon to receive a sudden shock. After his son was put back to bed the hectic flush on his cheeks became more marked, his eyes assumed a dreamy, faraway look, and he lay panting and breathless.

"Granny," whispered the boy, "I am going to leave you. My mother, who went to the angels last year, often comes to see me. Last night she kissed me ever so often, and when she left me she was beckoning me to follow her. Next time she comes I know she will take me with her."

"O, my wee lambie, ye'll no' gang an' leave your auld granny. If ye were awa' I wad hae nae freen' in a' the warld, an' oh! I'd be lanely withoot ye."

"But I'll come and kiss you and father like what mother did to me last night. Won't that be nice?" and the little fellow clapped his hands in delight at the prospect. Seeing Janet Rendal in tears, he continued— "Why are you crying, granny? Do you not remember how you told me to be a good boy after mother went away, and you always said that she would come for me some day? Didn't you tell me that mother's new home above the stars was far prettier and better than this one here? Why, then, are you now sorry that I am going to the Better Land to be with mother and the angels?"

"I'm not sorry, lambie, but we will miss you sairly, and, and——." The poor woman broke down and was unable to complete her sentence.

"Father will be your friend instead of me—won't you?" said the child, appealing with an earnest look to his father.

Gilbert Sandie was a strong-minded man, but the scene which he had just been witnessing was too much for him. He, an elder of the kirk, had thought the child was too young to be told of heavenly things, but this old woman whom he had persecuted for a lifetime had been doing the work for him. He had denounced her to the Session as one holding intercourse with the Evil One, and all the time she had been telling his darling of Him who said "Suffer the little children to come unto Me, . . . for of such is the kingdom of God." Truly the Spitting Witch had heaped coals of fire on his head.

Approaching the bed on which the dying boy lay, the father assured him that Janet Rendal would never be lonely again if he could help it, and he emphasised the words by grasping the woman's hand in his own. A happy smile spread over the child's face; and turning to Janet Rendal he whispered, "Granny, you have got a friend now; and when you get as tired and wearied as I am, I will come and kiss you like what mother did to me, and accompany you to our Happy Home."

The child shortly afterwards fell asleep, his father and Janet Rendal keeping watch by his bedside.

As the sun began to sink behind Rendall hills, bathing the landscape in a halo of crimson and gold, the old woman reverently imprinted a kiss upon the child's forehead, then turning to the father murmured, "Laird, see what a heavenly smile is on our wee lambie's face. Did you hear him whisper 'mother'. Ah, he's wi' her noo, an' wha kens but that the dazzling licht that's flashin' o'er hill an' dale marks the path o' God's chariot conveyin' his ransomed soul to glory."

When it became known that the laird of Isbister's only child was dead, and that the Spitting Witch was the only one present with him when the death took place, the news caused something like a sensation in the parish of Rendall. Everybody knew of the old-standing feud between the two families; and when it was remembered what an attraction Rigga had for the child, it was at once concluded that the poor little fellow's death had been brought about by foul means. The laird was urged on all hands to have the Spitting Witch tried for practising the black arts, but to the surprise of all, he maintained that she had proved herself a true friend, and that he was determined to support her as long as she lived.

Believing that he had been bewitched by his old enemy, his acquaintances resolved to have her tried for witchcraft, and they soon secured sufficient evidence of cattle and horses dying, of people going mad, and such like, to induce the authorities to take up the case.

The Spitting Witch was tried at Kirkwall on 11th November, 1629. After all the witnesses had been examined for the prosecution, the laird of Isbister spoke on her behalf, telling what she had done for his child, maintaining that she was a poor harmless woman who would not injure man nor beast, and earnestly urging that she should be set free. But it would have been better if he had not interfered, for the superstitious jurymen, knowing as they did how bitter he had previously been against the woman himself, accepted his defence of her now as fresh proof that he had been bewitched by the prisoner.

They found the poor woman guilty, and the sentence passed upon her was that she was to be taken to the Gallows Ha', Kirkwall, next day, there to be worried at the stake and her body to be burnt to ashes.

When Janet Rendal arrived at the place of execution on the following day, the laird of Isbister was at her side. As the rope was being adjusted round her neck, she turned, and in a low voice whispered, "Laird, last night oor wee lambie cam' an' kissed me as he promised, an' I can see him beckonin' on me noo. He'll also do as much for you, when you are nearing the end o' your journey in this vale o' tears."

But before she could say anything further by way of farewell, the hangman tightened the rope and she expired, a victim to the superstition of the times.

TWO RENDALL WITCHES

A great sensation was caused in Orkney in the beginning of the seventeenth century by the mysterious disappearance of a young woman named Mary Linklater, who resided in the parish of Rendall. Some held that she had been murdered by her lover, Thomas Irvine, but the popular feeling was that she had been wafted away to another world by the "devilrie" of the two parish witches, Kitty Grieve and Mary Richart.

On the night of the 26th February, 1600, Mary Linklater and Thomas Irvine, who were engaged to be married, were seen crossing the moor arm in arm, in the direction of Howan Greeny. That mound had always had an evil reputation. People coming home late at night, especially if they had been indulging in strong home-brewn ale, had often beheld mysterious lights floating about, and dances being performed by creatures who were not of this world.

A sensational story handed down was of three Evie men who had gone to Kirkwall on business by sea, but who, owing to severe weather, had to return by land. Each carried a sack on his back. It was dark when they were passing Howan Greeny, and on looking in they saw fairies dancing. One of the men determined to have a reel with the "trows," and he rushed in amongst them. He danced so long that his companions outside got impatient; but the only answer he would give them when asked to go home with them was, "Wait till the reel's ended." At length the two men left their friend behind. Two years afterwards, however, they had occasion to pass Howan Greeny, and upon looking inside they found their old companion still dancing with the fairies. They addressed him, when he exclaimed, "Bless me, have you not gone home yet!" They asked him to come out, but receiving the old answer—"Wait till the reel's ended"—they at once proceeded inside and pulled him out of the charmed circle.

But to return to our story. When last seen the young couple seemed to be on the best of terms with each other. Mary Linklater, however, was never seen to leave the moor, and no trace of her could afterwards be found. Nor could her lover give any satisfactory information regarding her disappearance. When informed next day that she had not returned to her father's house, he explained that he had parted with her nearly half-way across the moor. He said he was anxious to accompany her home as usual, but she absolutely refused to allow him to do so. She would, however, give him no reason for her strange behaviour, and he stated that when he tried to frighten her with references to Howan Greeny, in the hope that she would allow him to accompany her home, she laughingly retorted that she would perhaps get a dance with some of the "wee folk," which would more than compensate her for the loss of the walk with him.

On the other hand, Kitty Grieve and Mary Richart, the reputed witches, were seen at Howan Greeny on the night that Mary Linklater disappeared. A servant lad named James Frishell alleged that he heard a cry of murder in the direction of Howan Greeny, which was at once stifled. The night was dark, and he could see no distance out into the moor. However, he cautiously crept towards the haunted mound, and by and by he could hear some people engaged in a whispered conversation. At first he could only catch portions of sentences, but these were of such a character that he resolved at all hazards to get within hearing distance. He could then make out the figures of two women—these were the witches Kitty Grieve and Mary Richart—and also a tall man, black and indistinct as a shadow.

"Don't ask us to do it," he heard Kitty Grieve exclaim. "Already people credit us with holding communication with the Evil One, and what would become of us if this were known?"

"Who dare lift a finger to injure you so long as you have my protection?" asked the stranger.

"That may be so, my lord, but do not ask us to do this revolting work. We will do everything possible in the future, as we have done in the past, to carry out your commands, but do spare us on this occasion."

"And what say you, Richart, to this proposal? Have you also got squeamish over such trifles?"

"You know we are your lordship's slaves," was the reply. "Hitherto we have given up body and soul to your service, so that we are now as outcasts in our native parish, being shunned by old and young alike. We would rather—"

"O, give over this prating," broke in the stranger. "You have had your reward for all that you have done. Throughout the past months, when others were starving, you and your families have been fed by me. The bad harvest has not affected you."

"We admit all you kindnesses, my lord," was Kitty Grieve's answer. "But if I had known the terrible price that I would be called upon to pay for my daily bread, I should have preferred death to it."

"Boldly spoken, Kitty," was the sneering reply of the stranger; "but if death has so little terror for you, why try to avoid it? You have only to refuse to obey my command, and within a month the good people of Rendall will crowd to the hill over there to watch the flames devouring your bodies at the Gallows Ha' in Kirkwall. I give you both three minutes to decide you fate."

Frishell said the women burst into tears at the conclusion of this speech, whilst the stranger walked away a short distance.

Returning shortly afterwards the stranger demanded in an angry tone, "Will you obey, or do you prefer to end your lives at the stake as two rank and notorious witches?"

Frishell could not catch the answer given by Grieve and Richart, but he concluded that they had resolved to obey their hard taskmaster from the fact that the trio shortly afterwards left the mound of Howan Greeny and proceeded across the moor, where he lost sight of them. He then crept cautiously up to the mound, but he found little there to satisfy his curiosity. At one place he picked up what is locally known as a "caisie," in which was a large quantity of black oatmeal. Near by, he discovered a woollen shawl and a bit of blue worsted cloth, which had evidently been part of a woman's dress.

Something like a famine raged in Orkney at that time, owing to the failure of the harvest of the previous season, so that the find of oatmeal was considered a valuable one. He therefore resolved that he would await the return of the witches. Nearly two hours elapsed before the old women again put in an appearance, and Frishell afterwards confessed that the time appeared like an age, and was full of agony for him. At length, however, he saw the forms of the old women piercing the gloom, when he once more slipped into a hollow adjoining Howan Greeny.

The witches were now speaking in such low tones that he could make nothing of their conversation, so he boldly advanced from his hiding-place and demanded the name of the man with whom they had crossed the moor. The witches were apparently much annoyed when they found that their movements had been secretly watched.

Kitty Grieve, however, determined to brazen it out, and coolly answered that the man in black was the Evil One.

At a time when superstition was rife, and when the burning of witches was quite a common occurrence in Orkney, it is not surprising that this plain, unvarnished confession, considerably upset Frishell. He knew that both women, for some time previously, had been reputed witches. He had heard, too, of a farmer whose butter had gone wrong. He had sent to Kitty Grieve for some milk from her cow, and when it was put into his churn it produced eight pounds more than the proper quantity. Frishell therefore got frightened, and he left Howan Greeny with a rush, his pace being considerably quickened when he heard the mocking laughter of the witches.

Next day the whole parish knew of his adventure, and what added to the excitement was the fact that the shawl and piece of blue cloth found by Frishell were identified as having belonged to the missing girl, Mary Linklater. Information was promptly sent to Kirkwall, but for some reason or other the authorities there were very tardy in taking action, and when the women were at last apprehended the charge was not one of murder but of witchcraft.

Their trial took place in St Magnus Cathedral, Kirkwall, on 29th May, 1600. On the preceding day they were placed in the stocks at the Cross, when they were pelted with rubbish and derided by the inhabitants. Early in the afternoon, however, a strange priest appeared on the scene, who gave his protection to the two witches. His garb proclaimed his office, and when he ordered the crowd to stand back that he might have an opportunity of conversing with the prisoners the command was at once obeyed. After speaking long and earnestly in a low tone of voice to the culprits, he advised the people to leave the old women in peace till they were condemned.

At the trial quite a number of charges of witchcraft, sorcery, etc., were held by the jury to have been proved, but, to the surprise of everybody Mary Richart was dismissed with an admonition, whilst Kitty Grieve, who had first pled guilty and had then changed her mind, was sentenced to be taken to the Cross by the hangman, and to be publicly branded on the cheek with burning irons.

The judge gave as his reason for this unprecedented leniency in dealing with witchcraft the fact that both women were widows with large families, and that to have burned them at the stake would have been to jeopardise the lives of their children, especially at a time when the county was suffering from a severe famine, owing to the scarcity of grain.

Poor Kitty Grieve, however, did not long survive the brutal punishment meted out to her. She swooned whilst under the branding-iron of the hangman, and was subsequently conveyed to her home in Rendall a helpless invalid.

A few months later, when she saw that death was approaching, she sent for the parish clergyman to whom she made a confession in something like the following terms:— When a young woman she had been engaged as a nurse at the Earl's Palace in Kirkwall. An illegitimate son of Earl Patrick Stewart, on reaching manhood, had gone to the bad, and did a little piracy on his own account. He often came with his ship to Orkney for the purpose of robbing the people, as his father had done before him. The young man, during these visits, sometimes befriended his old nurse, Kitty Grieve, as well as her fellow servant, Mary Richart, but he had to get favours in return. These two women had to keep eyes and ears open, so that if they knew of any of their neighbours being in possession of valuables they conveyed the intelligence to him, who took an early opportunity thereafter of plundering them. It was known that Mary Linklater's father was a man of wealth, and it was suspected that his daughter was aware of the place where it was hidden. On the night of that young woman's disappearance, Kitty Grieve and Mary Richart persuaded her to meet them at Howan Greeny, on the pretence that they were to take her to an old person who was dying of starvation. Stewart was on the watch for her, and when he found that she would not tell where her father's valuables were secreted, he struck her on the head so violently with the back of his sword that he killed her on the spot, and afterwards forced Richart and Grieve to bury the body of the unfortunate young woman in the moss. Kitty Grieve further alleged that it was Stewart who, in the guise of a priest, had conversed with her companion and herself when they were in the stocks at Kirkwall Cross, and it was through his intervention that the judge was persuaded not to condemn them to be burnt at the stake. The reason why she was branded on the cheek was that she had threatened to make a confession regarding the murder, whilst Richart was let off because she was discreet enough to promise that she would say nothing that would call into question the actions of Stewart. Grieve admitted that she said to Frishell that she was in communication with the Evil One, and she still held that this was a faithful description of Stewart. She denied, however, that she ever had any supernatural gift such as witches were credited with possessing.

As this confession implicated a member of one of the first families in Orkney, an attempt was made to hush up the whole affair, and apparently no steps were taken to test its truth by trying to find the body.

However, it is said that murder will out, and in this case the body of Mary Linklater was found; but it was after the lapse of more than 250 years. and by a generation who knew nothing of the occurrences we have been referring to. The event was thus described in a paragraph which appeared in *The Orcadian* of 24th May, 1864, and goes far to prove the genuineness of the confession made by one of the reputed witches of Howan Greeny:

"On Saturday, 14th inst., James Craigie, while cutting peats in the moss about two and a half miles south-west from Burgar, came unexpectedly on a pair of shoes about four feet below the surface. Craigie saw enough to convince him that he had come on the remains of a human body, and he therefore abandoned his work, and went and informed his neighbours of his discovery. Intimation was sent to Kirkwall to the Procurator Fiscal, and Superintendent Grant went to Evie on Tuesday and sent some men to remove the turf which covered the remains. The body was that of a female. It was wrapped up in two petticoats of home manufacture, one black or blue, and the other of a brownish hue, which had probably been originally white, but had been dyed by the moss. The one petticoat was around the lower part of the body, the other had been cut up, laid under the upper part of the trunk and head, and then brought together in front and fastened by a piece of binding or trimming, passed through holes cut in the cloth, and tied round the head with a piece of brown worsted tape, woven, not knitted. A jacket or bodice, laced up in front with a woollen or worsted cord, was found under the petticoat which was round the upper part of the skeleton. Stockings, not knitted, but cut out of home-made stuff, and having a seam along the back, were on the legs. The shoes were of rough tanned leather, made somewhat similar to what are called 'turned pumps.' The soles were made of two folds of the same kind of leather which formed the upper part of the shoes. There was no other article of clothing found with the remains. The hair was brown . . . It is somewhat remarkable, as bearing on the preserving qualities of moss, that the woollen clothes and the hair were apparently little, if at all, injured. The brain also, in great measure, preserved its natural form, whilst the bones had become soft and spongy, and could easily be broken. The bones had, in short, been greatly changed, while the hair and wool had remained uninjured by the moss."

THE STORY OF THE ORKNEY CAT WITCH – A SANDAY TALE

In the good old days, when the municipal authorities in Orkney regulated the price and the quantity of the ale for the people, and when there was no restriction on private stills, a marvellous quantity of liquor was consumed in the course of an evening by the gentry at their convivial gatherings. The gentlemen of Sanday were specially famous because of the capacity they had for consuming whisky, and they generally would up their festivities with a mixture of boiling water, oatmeal, and strong spirits. This failing of theirs came to be so well known that they were at length named "gruelly-belkies"— a cognomen which has stuck to the natives of that crab-shaped island up to the present day.

One night in the winter of 1623, a number of Sanday gentlemen met in a house in the Burness district. They imbibed so heavily that many of the company fell under the table, and those who were able to retain their seats rolled about like ships in distress. One of those present—Thomas Logie—having an appointment, was forced to leave his friends about two o'clock in the morning. When he got outside, the cool air was so refreshing after the stifling atmosphere of the room he had just left, that he resolved to go home by Otterswick Bay. He knew this would add considerably to the length of his journey, but with this advantage that he would not have to pass the graveyard in Lady Parish—which, in these times, when ghosts and apparitions made their appearance almost nightly, was always a consideration. As he staggered along in the bracing frosty air, whistling to keep his courage up, he did not at all feel easy in mind. It had begun to dawn upon him that in taking such a roundabout way to avoid the home of the dead, he was approaching ground that was in much more evil repute.

The point of Coliness was just ahead; and, if all tales which he had heard were true, many a strange fairy dance had been witnessed there. He gazed anxiously towards the mound, which is quite a prominent feature in the landscape, and was considerably alarmed to behold what looked like pillars of smoke rising from beyond it, out of which electric streamers jutted up after each other in bewildering profusion, spreading themselves over the whole northern sky. If Thomas had been sober he would have attributed this phenomenon to a grand display of aurora borealis, but as it was, he concluded that the scene had something supernatural in it. However, to have turned back would have been cowardly, and in addition he felt that his legs were too unsteady to carry him at the pace he would like to travel in beating such a retreat.

He therefore came to a standstill. All at once, there fell
upon his ears a series of unearthly yells, which resembled
nothing so much as the screams of a child in dire distress.
Thomas dropped on the ground limp, helpless and considerably
sobered. By and by he could see that the mound was covered
with a crowd of little moving objects, whose eyes vengefully
sparkled and gleamed like balls of fire. Having crossed himself,

he adjured them to give over their evil work. For answer, one of the spiteful trows spat at him, and the others made the bay resound with their mocking laughter, which caused him to quiver in every limb. Whilst his gaze was fixed on the strange creatures, they assumed the forms of cats, the largest one—which, according to Logie's own statement, was perfectly black, and the size of a small native pony—having the face of an old woman named Annie Taylor.

He had heard that an infallible means of protecting people from the wiles of witches and fairies was to go backwards thrice round the ground occupied by the spirits, repeating the words, "I have kissed the Holy Book." He therefore mustered sufficient courage to put this old saying to the test; but he somehow got out of the circle and walked straight into the little loch of stagnant water which lies in the vicinity. As he fell full length into it, however, he yelled so lustily for help that the strange occupants of the mound speedily disappeared. Some of the people at the farm of Colliegarth happened to hear the noise, ran down to his assistance, helped him to his feet, and were regaled with an account of his adventure as given above.

When this story became current over the island, an old woman, Annie Taylor, was at once dubbed the Cat Witch. This character suited her admirably. Where she had come from no one knew. When first seen in Sanday a few years previously she was carrying a "caisie" on her back, and it was positively asserted that all it contained was a cat and a few kittens. She took possession of an empty hut in the parish of Cross, evidently without leave, and no one cared to call in question her title to it.

In the autumn of 1624 a great cock-fight took place at Backaskaill, Sanday. There was a tremendous crowd of people present to witness the brutal sport, amongst these being Captain Sinclair, a gentleman who represented himself as a naval officer, and who was said to be visiting the island for the purpose of marrying the daughter of the Laird of Silver Ha'. During a lull in the proceedings Captain Sinclair, with one or two friends, had left the ring and was leisurely parading up and down the links enjoying the bracing sea breezes.

Annie Taylor happened then to be passing along the outskirts of the crowd, and Captain Sinclair, who had apparently been told that she was proficient in the occult sciences, crossed over to her and demanded with a supercilious air whether she could read his fortune. Annie Taylor gave a sudden start at the sound of his voice, then gazed long and earnestly into his face. He did not seem to appreciate this scrutiny, and petulantly repeated his question.

"Perhaps I could tell you something of your history", was the reply of the old woman, "but I would rather do so in privacy."

"But you don't expect me to believe that an ignorant old person such as you can tell anything that is likely to be of any interest to me."

"Put me to the test," and so saying she whispered a single word into his ear.

Captain Sinclair no sooner heard it than he bounded from her side, muttering "Devil." But he speedily recovered himself, blandly said he would like to have his fortune told, and that he would be glad to meet her for that purpose.

That same night he called at Annie Taylor's humble abode. He entered the house without any ceremony, assuming a very swaggering air as he did so. "Now, you old reptile," said he, as he divested himself of his cloak, "I have come to this place of yours to hear what you know about that name you mentioned at Backaskaill this afternoon."

Annie Taylor, without venturing a reply, proceeded to trim an old Orcadian Lamp, which consisted of two rudely-formed shallow metal basins, the oil burning in them having been extracted from small fish, and a few dried rashes doing duty for a wick.

"Come on, you old fiend,' exclaimed Sinclair impatiently, "and tell me who this Gray is that you flouted in my face at the sports today."

"Thomas Gray," calmly replied Annie Taylor, "now goes under the name of Captain Sinclair, and, though his wife is still living, he is trying to secure the hand and fortune of the young lady of Silver Ha'."

"You lie," angrily exclaimed her visitor, nervously fingering his sword, " and I have a good mind to rid the world of your ugly carcase. Where is the proof that I am a married man?

Standing erect and tearing off her headgear, Annie Taylor was no longer the old woman that she had pretended to be. "Do you know your wife now, Thomas Gray?" she asked with flashing eyes.

The change was so sudden and complete that Sinclair sprang backwards towards the door showing every symptom of terror. Recovering himself, however, he drew his sword and began to advance, evidently with the intention of attacking the woman.

"Stop," she commanded. "When I agreed to meet you to-night, I made such preparations as would enable me to defend myself against the attack of a coward. Advance another step, and I have only to drop this lamp into the barrel of powder at my side to put an end to your wicked career."

A glance at the barrel indicated, at once cowed Sinclair, who stood in the middle of the floor checkmated and crestfallen. Annie Taylor then continued, "You little expected to see your wife here. Ten years ago, when your correspondence with your Sanday sweetheart fell into my hands, and you plunged a dagger into my breast, you left me for dead; and, under your assumed name of Captain Sinclair, you thought, I suppose, that you could never be tracked." The woman seemed to be labouring under deep emotion, which so overpowered her that she was unable to complete her sentence.

Sinclair, seeing this, broke in with the question: "And what does my wife wish now that she has got me in her den?"

"I have prayed and laboured for years for such a meeting as this, in my desire to have my revenge for all I have suffered at your hands, and now I recoil from the crime of murder; but I can, at least, save that innocent young woman up at Silver Ha' from such a fate as mine has been."

"How?" interrupted Sinclair.

"By making terms with you," was the calm reply.

"And if I refuse?"

"I drop this lamp into the powder keg, and we shall leave this world together in smoke and flames," was the prompt answer; and suiting the action to the word, she brought the spluttering and burning oil so near the explosive that Sinclair visibly blanched.

"Now," continued Annie Taylor, "you promise that you leave this island immediately, and will never enter into correspondence again with the young lady at Silver Ha', or your wicked career ends here and now."

Sinclair saw that the woman was quite earnest enough to put her threat into execution, so that he at once gave the necessary promise.

Annie Taylor then withdrew the lamp from the vicinity of the powder, and, with a contemptuous wave of the arm, added, "You may go now," turning her back upon him as an indication that so far as she was concerned the interview was over.

Sinclair lost no time in getting outside of the door, when he gave vent to the enigmatical assertion, "Smoke and flames, my dear, may be used by a wicked husband as well as by an outraged wife."

*   *   *

Anyone passing through Kirkwall one day about three months after the event related above could have seen that the inhabitants were labouring under some great excitement. The narrow, tortuous streets, running in a semi-circle from the harbour at the north end of the town to Scapa Road on the other side, were crowded with people in holiday attire. By eleven o'clock in the forenoon the centre of attraction seemed to be Broad Street, and around St Magnus Cathedral was a noisy, surging crowd all intent upon getting admission to the ancient minster. There was no Court House in the capital of the Orkneys in those days, and the Cathedral was used not only for public worship, but as a place for conducting the more important of the criminal trials from all parts of the county.

On this occasion, the unfortunate woman to be tried was Annie Taylor, the charge against her being that of witchcraft; and though such cases were by no means rare in Orkney in the seventeenth century, they were always very "popular"— the inhabitants making a special point of being present to witness the proceedings. Sir John Buchanan of Spottiswood having taken his seat as Judge, the woman was asked to plead.

In a clear, firm voice she declared she was innocent of the charge brought against her, a statement which was greeted with loud hisses. Proof was then led.

Mary Scott deponed that she had asked the prisoner how she might prevent anyone taking the "profit" from her cow, and was told to pluck three hairs from as many different parts of the animal's body, go thrice "wonderwardis" round the beast stroking it on the left side. This having been accomplished, the hairs were to be cast into the churn, and the following words were to be repeated over and over again: "Come, butter, come." After doing that, witness declared that she never afterwards lost the "profit" of her cow.

Benjamin Tulloch said he was once very sick, and his friends sent for the accused, who cured him. She did it in this way. She put her hands alternately on his head, his feet, and his heart, saying, "Mother's blessing to the head, mother's blessing to the feet, and mother's blessing to the heart." These words had not been well pronounced, said the witness, when he was able to rise from his bed, strong and well.

Thomas Muir alleged that the prisoner went to his house at Quoykankeris one day and told him if he went down to the beach he would find fish. He went and got a large whale.

Elspeth Peace stated that she accused the prisoner on one occasion of taking some peats from her. Annie Taylor denied this, and told the witness she would rue making such a charge. And she did, for owing to the witchcraft of the accused the tide came up and swept the whole of her peats away.

Thomas Logie also appeared and gave an account of his experience of the prisoner's witchcraft as had come under his own observation at the Point of Coliness, on the occasion already referred to.

This was all the evidence led against the accused, and is taken almost verbatim from the official documents of the Court.

The verdict was that the prisoner was not guilty of transforming herself into a cat, it being, no doubt, concluded that Logie was too drunk when he had the adventure to give a reliable account of what he had seen. It was considered, however, that the rest of the evidence was quite sufficient to show that Annie Taylor was a rank witch.

The Judge then sentenced the unfortunate woman to be taken next day from the prison to the Gallows Ha', there to be worried at a stake, and her body to be burnt to ashes.

When this terrible sentence was pronounced, the immense crowd which filled the Cathedral raised a joyful cheer, showing that they had no sympathy with the poor wretch whose life was to be offered up as a sacrifice to their superstitions.

The prisoner was then led to the condemned cell, which was situated in the tower of the Cathedral.

Shortly after the Curfew bell had rung, the streets of Kirkwall were deserted. Not a light was to be seen, and even the stars were hidden behind a dark, impenetrable cloud. No sound broke the awful silence, even the sea crept in on the beach on this particular night without a murmur or a moan.

About ten o'clock a muffled figure emerged from the Watergate—the passage which separates the Earl's Palace from the Bishop's Tower—and slowly groped across the graveyard to the south of the Cathedral. Having reached the side entrance, one loud and three light raps were given. Immediately afterwards the door was cautiously opened and Captain Sinclair hurriedly entered. It was evident that the hangman and his assistant (who had been deputed to watch the condemned woman during the last night she was to spend on earth) had been bribed by the visitor.

After a whispered consultation, Sinclair was ushered into the prisoner's cell, the others remaining outside. "Ah, my dear, you are coming near enough the smoke and flames now," was his sarcastic remark on getting face to face with the condemned woman.

Annie Taylor, who was sitting huddled up in a corner with her elbows on her knees, and her head thrown forward on her hands, did not show by the slightest movement that she had heard the cruel sneer.

Sinclair thereupon continued, "Ah, you are sulky because the tables have been turned upon you, my dear. You see that amongst my other accomplishments I have added that of a witch-maker. I suppose you would suspect, my dear, that it was at my request you were prosecuted, and that it was my money that provided the witnesses who have sworn your life away. As you reminded me in Sanday, steel could not take your life, and I am anxious now to see whether your body can resist fire."

Before the prisoner could reply to this brutal speech, the door of the cell was thrown open, and Sir John Buchanan, accompanied by two officers, entered.

"So it was you who hatched the plot to have Annie Taylor burnt as a witch?" asked the Judge in stern tones. "A merciful providence, however, has brought me to the prison cell in time to hear your confession, and this poor woman will now be set free. You will therefore take her place here."

"On what charge?" tremblingly asked the bully.

"Piracy on the high seas," was the reply.

On hearing these words Sinclair looked aghast, but, recovering himself, began to protest his innocence.

"Silence," shouted Sir John. "There is no hope of your escape. That night you went to get your fortune told by your wife here, the lady of Silver Ha' heard sufficient of what was stated at the interview to arouse her suspicions regarding you. Her subsequent inquiries were so well conducted that your connection with the pirate schooner Lizzie Jane was traced, and that vessel with all its crew has now been captured in Inganess Bay. All we require to make the seizure complete was the pirate captain, and he has been so obliging as to walk into prison of his own accord. What say you to that, Thomas Gray?"

The pirate was so taken by surprise at this new turn of affairs that he was speechless

When Annie Taylor, or, as we should now call her, Mrs Gray, saw the noose so unexpectedly but surely tightening around her husband, she forgot all her own injuries, threw herself at the feet of Sir John Buchanan and pled that some mercy should be shown to the culprit.

"Mercy!" ejaculated the Judge. "Let him look for it above, for he deserves none, and will get none, when he comes before my Court to be tried for his misdeeds."

The Judge, officers, and Mrs Gray then left the cell. The wretched man was never seen alive again. That night the tower of St Magnus Cathedral was struck by lightning, and one of the large stones which fell inwards crashed through the roof of the prison cell, killing Gray on the spot.

When the facts of the case became known, much sympathy was aroused in favour of Mrs Gray, and witch-hunting was then as vehemently denounced as it had previously been applauded. The result was that the last woman tried in an Orkney Court on a charge of sorcery was Annie Taylor, the Cat Witch.

A ROMANCE OF THE STONES OF STENNESS

" Are sweethearts for eating, grandma?"
This startling question was put by my little nephew, Johnnie Halcrow, a five-year-old youngster who was the plague and the spoiled darling of our household.

His mother died when he was an infant, his father went abroad, and wee Johnnie found a home with us in Birsay.

There were five of us at home before our wee pet arrived—

my father Benjamin Brough, my mother, my two sisters Jeannie and Bella, and myself.

Johnnie, naturally enough, was a spoiled child, and old-fashioned beyond his years, as the greater part of our spare time was spent in petting him.

I noticed that my sister Bella blushed scarlet when she heard Johnnie's question, and moved uneasily in her chair, as my mother, adjusting her spectacles, asked us what the bairn meant.

A painful silence ensued, and I was beginning to hope that the subject would be allowed to drop, when Johnnie, with the most innocent air in the world, clambered up on my mother's knee and threw his arms around her neck, which was always a preliminary with him when about to pitch a bombshell amongst us.

"Grandma," said he, "aren't the savages, who eat people, bad men?"

"Yes, dear, being cannibals they are just like wild beasts."

"Well," continued Johnnie, "I know a cannibal who lives quite close to our house."

"Who is that?" asked my mother with an amused smile.

"It is David Stanger, the Laird of Lucknow," was Johnnie's prompt reply.

David Stanger owned the farm adjoining ours. His fair hair, blue eyes, ruddy complexion, all proclaimed his Norse descent; but, whatever he might have been in war, no one gave him credit for having much of the daring of his forebears in love affairs. Indeed, he was put down as being bashful to a fault in the presence of the fair sex, and we often twitted our sister Bella as to how he carried on his courtship.

When, therefore, little Johnnie uttered his name all eyes were turned towards Bella, whose face at this particular moment was a study. Though she bent closely over her knitting to hide the tell-tale blushes which overspread her countenance, the younger members of the family were quite aware of the agony she was enduring.

My mother, who had a strong liking for Stanger stoutly defended him as one of the best young men in the parish, and ordered Johnnie to tell why he described him as a cannibal.

"Well," said Johnnie. "I heard him ask our Bella if she would be his sweetheart, and when she said she would, he told her he liked her so well he could eat her!"

It is needless to say that Johnnie's remarks drove my sister from the room, while my mother was only able to ejaculate, "Was there ever such a boy as this?"

As for Johnnie, he began to scamper about with our dog Ginger, apparently quite oblivious of the sensation which his speech had caused.

How Johnnie had got his information was a mystery to us all, because courtship as it is practised in Orkney is rather a mysterious affair, and is rarely indulged in openly. When a young man leaves home to visit his sweetheart he may be depended upon to go in an easterly direction if she lives in the west, at least so long as he is in his own neighbourhood. In short, courtship is always indulged in on the sly.

After the old people have gone to bed the daughter prepares to receive her lover. A good supply of peats having been thrown on the fire, the girl unbolts the door, places a light near the window (which is a common signal that the coast is clear), and then awaits the arrival of her young man, who generally makes his appearance in his stocking soles, with his boots under his arm.

Young ministers, when they first arrive in the county and hear of this state of affairs, are not slow to denounce it from the pulpit. They even approach the parents privately to get their assistance in putting it down. But old people are the strongest defenders of the ancient practice. We did it ourselves, they say, and never saw any harm in it, and so they decline to interfere in the matter.

My sister's courtship had probably been carried on in this way, but though we had a strong suspicion of the fact, Johnnie's prattle came upon us very much as a revelation.

A few weeks later we had fresh proof of this clandestine courtship on the part of my sister. We received it in a startling, not to say alarming manner. It was Christmas eve; we had retired to rest early, as is the custom in Orkney, and were awakened about midnight by a series of screams, mingled with which was the angry barking of our dog.

Having got a light I rushed to the passage. I will not soon forget the scene being enacted there.

Near the front door was David Stanger, jumping about like a madman, emitting a moan each time his feet touched the floor, while my sister Bella, three or four yards away, was performing similar evolutions, and screaming loudly.

All this was bad enough, but when my father, a douce elder of the kirk, who prided himself upon the thorough control he had over his temper and feelings, came out to the passage and performed similar antics, I began to think that everybody in the house had suddenly became demented.

With the assistance of the light I brought into the passage Stanger ultimately managed to find his way out of the house, and I noticed that, as he passed through the doorway, he threw a peculiar glance of mingled shame and indignation at my sister.

Bella then hurriedly retired and the passage was thus left in possession of my father and myself.

After muttering some words which struck me as being much stronger than should be used by anyone in the eldership, my father went down on his knees and closely examined into the cause of the mischief.

"Well," said he, as he got on his feet again, "if that does not beat everything! Somebody has been spreading thistles along the whole length of the passage!"

Though my father had good cause to feel annoyed at the disturbance which had deprived him of his rest, not to speak of the agony he had endured by the prickling of the thistles, he was now so tickled by the ludicrousness of the situation, that he actually laid his back against the wall and indulged in a hearty fit of laughter.

Next morning, when we sat down to breakfast, no mention was made of the exciting events of the previous night. But, all the same, the meal was a most uncomfortable one. We were very quiet, and my sister Bella might have been described as "sheep-faced." She never lifted her head.

Little Johnnie, as was usual on such occasions, broke the spell. "Grandma," said he? "did you ever see Santa Claus?"

"No, dear, he does not care to make the acquaintance of old people. He loves good little boys best."

"No, grandma, he loves the lasses far better than the boys.
"What makes you think that, Johnnie?"

"Oh, last night I wanted to see what he was like, and I hid behind the meal girnal. He came in so quietly that I think he must have had wings; his feet never touched the floor—at least he made no noise. Aunt Bella was sitting on the straw-backed chair at the fire, and—"

My sister had evidently heard enough, for she rose from the table and bolted outside, my father remarking the lass looked as if she had taken leave of her senses.

Johnnie, after the interruption caused by the sudden exit of my sister, apparently forgot all about her and Santa Claus, and became engrossed in the contemplation of his egg.

My mother, whose curiosity had evidently been aroused, asked what Santa Claus did when he entered the house.

"Oh," said Johnnie, "he pulled Bella out of the chair, sat down on it himself, and took her on his knee. He saw my stockings hanging at the side of the fire, and he wanted to put sweeties in them; but aunt said that I was a little wretch, and that cinders were good enough for me. When he put the cinders into my stockings I was vexed I could not get some in his, but I remember that I had a lot of thistles in the back kitchen that I had gathered to make a cushion for our teacher to sit on, and I slipped away and spread these upon the passage, so that Santa Claus would get them in his feet when he was going out. After I came back, Santa Claus told aunt I was a spoiled boy, and a rope's end would do me a lot of good. I did not like to hear him talking in that way about me, so I progged his leg with a darning needle, and afterwards pinched my aunt's arm. They did not know I was there, and they were angry with each other. Santa Claus said aunt was a cruel thing; and she said he was a monster, and that she would never speak to him again. Santa Claus then went out into the passage, and when he tramped on the thistles he roared like what the pigs do when they are getting killed. When aunt heard him making the noise she ran to help him, but he said she had made a fool of him, and that she would never get the chance to do so again. When aunt heard him say that, and felt the thistles prickling her feet, she screamed worse than Santa Claus did."

Here we had the explanation of the uproar which had roused us all out of bed the previous night, and though we ought to have punished little Johnnie for the part he had played in it, we were powerless to do so. The comical nature of the story, and the innocent way it was told, were amply sufficient to secure for him a free pardon.

We, of course, knew that Santa Claus seen by Johnnie was the young Laird of Lucknow. What we could not make out, however, was whether Johnnie's ignorance was real or assumed.

After this, my sister Bella could not be induced, on any occasion, to discuss the subject of Santa Claus's visit; and, as for the laird, he did not come near the house again.

My sister Jeannie and myself, when we happened to meet him, sometimes tried to draw him out by asking for his poor feet, but he dexterously parried all thrusts of that kind, and left us in the dark as to what his sentiments were regarding the matter. If Johnnie's version of the dispute was the correct one, we had little doubt that the breach between the lovers would soon be healed, but in this we were disappointed, as the sequel will show.

* * *

Ten years after the events related above, my sister Bella and David Stanger remained as distant as ever. On the rare occasions when they happened to meet they barely recognised each other as they passed.

But, notwithstanding this, we were satisfied that they had by no means forgotten the courtship of their younger years. Neither, so far as could be seen, ever indulged in idle flirtation, and the painful way they blushed when they met, along with their awkward attempts to assume a coolness which they apparently did not feel, was convincing proof to onlookers that they only required to be brought together in a favourable position to give and receive such explanations as would lead to a happy reconciliation.

The opportunity at length occurred. There was to be a marriage in Stenness, to which a very large company was invited. When our family arrived, we found that Stanger was there before us.

When the marriage ceremony was over and the company were being paired for supper, I kept a special eye on Bella and the laird of Lucknow, and I was rather pleased to see that that young gentleman was always within easy distance of my sister. The result of this was that they were partnered for the supper table.

But neither seemed to be happy during the supper-hour, and I noticed that they were very restrained in their conversation.

My nephew, Johnnie, who was now a tall, handsome boy of fifteen, sat opposite my sister and her old sweetheart, and his eyes were dancing with mischief. On the few occasions that Bella ventured to lift her gaze from the table, she had to face the grimaces of my nephew, who, in a twinkling, could assume the serious air that Stanger generally put on of late years in presence of my sister, and could change it as rapidly to that of the mock grief which a broken-hearted maiden might be supposed to feel.

When supper was over, the news was sent round that the company was to form into pairs for the marriage march.

This old custom, which though falling into desuetude of late in Orkney, except, perhaps in outlying districts, was always indulged in at the time of our story, and to have left out the parade from the bride's house to the Parish Kirk and back would have deprived a marriage of one of the most attractive features of the ceremony, at least in the eyes of the younger people.

However, at the time of which I write, this old custom was in full vogue. We were ranged in couples, the fiddlers leading the way, playing that favourite tune of the Orcadians on such occasions, "I'll make the bride come follow me now."

The night was a lovely one. Away on the northern horizon was an immense bank of black cloud, from which the aurora borealis continually flashed, throwing out myriads of streamers and lighting up the whole sky with a brilliancy almost equalling moonlight.

The march round the church was, in these circumstances, accompanied amid much hilarity, so that when we returned the company was in great good humour.

There was one exception, however. My sister refused to join in the dance, and she appeared white and scared, as if labouring under some great excitement. Thinking a whiff of fresh air might revive her, I got her persuaded to come outside. The merry dancers had by this time disappeared, heavy clouds swept across the sky, and everything was draped in darkness.

"What a night to visit the Stone of Odin," I heard my sister mutter as she gazed away in the direction of the Standing Stones of Stenness. Then, putting her arm round my waist, she continued, "The Spirit of Woden demands my presence at the Temple of the Moon tonight!"

"You are joking, Bella," I replied, though I knew quite well by the shudder which accompanied her remarks that she was only too serious.

"Joking?" said she. "Who dare trifle with Woden? Three nights in succession his spirit has appeared to me in the shape of a miniature moon, and this evening you saw his messengers the merry dancers, beckoning me to meet him at his temple at the midnight hour!"

Around the peat-fires of Orkney during the long winter evenings, old people revel in relating such anecdotes as have a smack of the supernatural about them, and in the West Mainland especially, the god Woden has ever been a favourite with the gossip.

Woden was always described to us as the friend of lovers—making love's rugged path straight for them—and my sister had accurately described the method tradition said he took of summoning people to his presence.

I tried to persuade her that she must be labouring under some sort of delusion, but without effect. She implicitly believed she had received a summons from Woden, and I was alarmed to find that, at all hazards, she was determined that night to visit the Temple of the Moon, one of the outlying sentinels of the famous Standing Stones of Stenness.

Seeing I was powerless to dissuade her from undertaking what I considered a very foolhardy journey, I afterwards appealed to Stanger for advice. To my surprise, he told me that he had also seen the Spirit of Odin thrice, and that he intended to obey the summons.

I then arranged that I should accompany my sister and that he should follow at a little distance so that she should not see him, whilst he would be near enough to render assistance if that were needed.

About half-past eleven o'clock I noticed my sister stealing away from the company, and I followed. At first she objected to my company, but, as I insisted that I should go with her, she ultimately gave way to me.

Even in the daylight the place has something uncanny about it. The Standing Stones of Stenness—mouldering, scarred and grey with age—rising as they do from an unbroken bed of heather, always have a weird, mysterious appearance. The sparkling of the water in Loch Stenness on one side of the promontory on which they stand, and the well-cultivated green fields of the one hundred lairds of Harray stretching out on the other, and sloping away up the hill towards Rendall, help to accentuate the eternal gloom which hangs over those monuments of a barbaric age.

The memory of our midnight journey to this weird and mystic circle will go with me to the grave. Not a human habitation was near, and in my then excited frame of mind, the whins and bracken growing along the sides of the road assumed the most horrible and fantastic shapes. The silence was intense, being broken only by the restless water of the loch rising and falling, which sounded like heavy, crunching footsteps; or the scream of a sea-bird overhead—which appeared to me like the wailing of a lost spirit.

As we passed the Bridge of Brodgar, and could dimly see the Standing Stones of Stenness on the eminence beyond—looming in the darkness like a regiment of grim spectres—an indescribably creepy feeling took possession of me, and I would have given worlds to get my sister to return.

But she wouldn't. Let the ordeal cost what it might, she said she was determined to go through with it.

As we approached the Stone of Odin it appeared to be larger and more unshapely than usual, and all the ghastly traditions associated with it flashed through my mind with the most perplexing persistence. I could see the human victims being led up to it. I saw their struggles as they were being tied to the hole running through it and I imagined I beheld them being offered as a sacrifice to Woden. Though the perforation in this stone was now used for a very different purpose—for lovers to clasp each other's hands in while plighting their troth—it was only the harrowing associations connected with it that forced themselves upon me.

After a little hesitation, we advanced a few paces, when further progress was arrested on my part by a blood-curdling sight. Right in front of the Stone of Odin we could see the outline of a human skull, with a half-moon above it. The horrid thing flashed and sparkled just as the aurora borealis had done in the heavens a few hours previously. I clutched my sister's arm, and would have screamed if I had had the power; but my voice was gone.

Bella stood irresolute for a few minutes, then saying in a hoarse whisper. "Woden must be obeyed," she advanced. As for myself, I dropped on the heather limp and helpless.

When Bella got quite close to the Stone of Odin I was startled to hear her addressed by an invisible presence:

"Woden welcomes you to the Temple of the Moon. The courage which has enabled you to come at the midnight hour to this lonely spot, guarded as it is by the spirits and monuments of long-past generations, gives evidence that the blood of your Norse fathers courses through your veins. Woden wishes to befriend you, and in return you must take his vow. Are you willing?"

My sister's answer did not reach me, but it must have been satisfactory, as the invisible one added: "Down on your knees. Think now of him whom you would have for a life-partner, and I will summon him at once to this our temple."

From where I was lying I could see my sister kneeling, and by and by the silence was again broken by the same voice.

"All things are known to Woden. Stanger, approach and meet thy fate."

As these words were uttered, David Stanger suddenly made his appearance, and my sister probably labouring under the combined feelings of terror and shame, rose to her feet, as if to fly from the awful ordeal.

"Stay," cried the invisible one. "In the presence of Woden

and your sweetheart nothing can harm you so long as you are obedient. Proceed now with your vow.

I then heard my sister's voice, and though I could not make out what she was saying, I knew she was asking, as so many of the fair daughters of Orkney had done in the past, that Woden might enable her to be true to the young man at her side.

"You must now go to the Temple of the Sun, where you, Stanger, will make a similar vow," was the next command.

Without a word the lovers rose from their knees, and crossed over to the Temple of the Sun.

When they disappeared in the darkness I was struck with horror. I could not lift my eyes from the hideous skull in front of the Stone of Odin, and the longer I looked the worse it grew. To my excited imagination it appeared to be moving spasmodically, the grin on the face expanding and contracting as regularly as if wrought by clockwork.

At one time I made up my mind to get rid of the horrible sight of the thing by making a rush along the road I had come, but I found this impossible. The skull acted upon me like a magnet and I could not turn my back upon it.

Relief, however, came at last. Across the moor, in the direction of the Temple of the Sun, I could make out the shadowy forms of the lovers returning, and it cost me a terrible struggle to refrain from rushing over to meet them.

As they took up their position in front of the Stone of Odin again, they were thus addressed:

"Both of you know that a love-vow, taken in presence of Woden, is inviolable. Being aware of this, are you willing to plight your troth here in the same way as your fathers and mothers have done in the past?"

In the calm midnight air the affirmative answers of the lovers were distinctly carried to me.

"Clasp each other's right hand within the ring of Odin then, and repeat these words after me," was the next command. Then followed the words: "We hereby promise to be true and faithful to each other till death do us part. So help us, Woden."

Stanger afterwards rejoined my sister, and the hearty smack that followed told me that their long and foolish quarrel was now at an end.

The voice again broke the silence. "Woden is great, and he pities the weakness of lovers. Because wee Johnnie Halcrow progged your leg with a needle ten years ago, Stanger, you parted with your sweetheart. The same wee boy pinched your arm, Bella, and you took the huff at a man who would have gone through fire and water for you; and, had it not been for the interference of Woden, false pride would still have kept you apart. Go home now, and may the experience of the past keep you from being guilty of such follies in the future, as have made your lives miserable in recent years."

It was Stanger's time to speak now, and his remarks, to me, at least, were rather startling.

"Come down, Johnnie," said he. "You have played Woden very well."

In answer to the summons I saw a dark object drop from the summit of the stone, followed by a merry peal of laughter on the part of my nephew. Stanger then added, "The happiness you have given me tonight, Johnnie, prevents me from visiting you with that condign punishment which your ill-timed pranks merit."

Johnnie jumped round the pair chaffing and laughing, and I could hear Bella exclaim as she buried her head on Stanger's shoulder, "Oh, Davie, what asses we have made of ourselves!"

Bella and Stanger returned to the marriage company together, whilst Johnnie and I followed more leisurely. I then learned that my mischievous nephew, knowing as he did the traditions regarding Woden, had drawn a miniature moon on our byre with phosphorus at times when it could easily be seen by my sister, so as to get her to go to the Stone of Odin. He told me further that the skull which had been such a terror to me was also his work.

Stanger and my sister eighteen months later gave the best possible proof that they had forgiven my nephew for the pranks he had played upon them by having their son and heir christened "John Halcrow."

As for my nephew, you would have some difficulty in believing that he, who became a popular minister in one of our city churches, was in his early days the plague of our house, and also the sham god Woden.

PART IV—NOTABLE ORCADIANS

THE REV. JOHN GERARD

One wild blustering night many winters ago a number of neighbours had gathered around a rousing peat-fire in the Herston district of South Ronaldsay. The conversation, as was quite natural, brought up the name of the Rev. John Gerard. One of the company, looking across the fire at old Watty Sinclair, asked that worthy whether he knew this once famous minister.

Slowly laying aside his pipe, and gazing at his questioner with open-eyed amazement at his ignorance (whether assumed or otherwise we need not stay to enquire), Watty exclaimed—"Did I know Mr Gerard? Man, you might as well have asked if I know my own wife or my own bairns. A more sensible question would have been, Is there anybody in South Ronaldsay or in Orkney that has not heard of him?"

It was quite plain that Watty was very much out of temper because such ignorance had been imputed to him. He had well-nigh worshipped Mr Gerard in life and now that the eccentric old minister was gathered to his fathers, Watty would gladly have transformed him into an Orkney saint.

Mansie Louttit, who was a man of tact, and was well aware of his old friend's peculiarities, mildly suggested that it would be well if the rising generation knew more of Mr Gerard than they did; and he was sure there was no one in Orkney better fitted to give that gentleman's biography than Watty Sinclair.

This bit of flattery somewhat mollified Watty, and, as he was pressed by all present to tell the story of Mr Gerard's life-work in the county, he cleared his throat and began:—

"Well, Mr Gerard came to Orkney in 1814, and for about fifteen years after was the only minister in South Ronaldsay and Burray. I think his parents were poor people, for he told me himself that the first money he earned was in herding cattle, and that he had to trim rushes for oily lamps to get possession of a pen-knife, when he was quite a child. But I know very little of his early history. However, I will say this, without fear of contradiction, that he was the best known minister in Orkney in his day. He was a good bit of a wag, and, as you know, the people in every parish in the county have something funny to relate regarding him. Judged by his sayings alone—and it is well to remember that he sometimes got credit for remarks he never made—it might be thought that he was a wild uncultivated man; but those who knew him best—both Churchmen and Dissenters—will admit that he was a Christian and a gentleman. He was certainly a terror to evil-doers, but he was very gentle and kind to children. There is no doubt he was odd in everything he did, and I for one could scarcely look in his face at any time without laughing. Some of his illustrations were so coarse that they are not fit to be repeated; but he always used these for the attainment of a good object. At a time when temperance was at a discount, Mr Gerard vehemently denounced the drinking customs of the people, and was a prominent member of the first temperance society formed in Orkney. He was an enthusiastic musician, and did much to stimulate a taste for music in the county. When he came to the parish the singing in his church was very bad, and in describing it to a friend he said—'A man had a book, and a man sang, but horrible was the music!' To remedy this state of matters he taught music classes in the different districts of his extensive parish, and in this way effected a great improvement in congregational singing. In connection with these classes he composed lines to be sung with the two different metres. The long metre was as follows:—

'Music religious thoughts inspires,
And kindles in us pure desires,
Gives pleasure to a well-tuned mind
The most exalted and refined.'

The common metre was:—
> 'Come let us sing the tune of French—
>> The second measure low—
> The third extendest very high
>> And the fourth down, down, doth go.'

"His originality and eccentricity of character will serve as a monument to him as durable as stone. He was a man of warm affection and upright principle, and while his piety would compare favourably with the professions of our modern clergy, his quaint and humorous traits of character and singular strength of intellect, marked him out as perhaps the most rare and gifted clergymen in Orkney during his generation.

"Mr Gerard gave so freely of his means to poor people, that he often ran short of change. On one occasion he had employed a rat-catcher, but was unable to pay him. He therefore presented him with a note in the following terms, to be delivered to Mr Thomas Budge of Brough:—'Manse, 13th August, 1849.—Dear Sir,—The bearer, William Duff, has this day given my large family of rats their LAST SUPPER! I have not 3s. to pay him. Keep this as your receipt, and give the poor man 3s. to help him over the Firth.—Yours truly, John Gerard.'

"Writing to Mr John Allan, Burwick, under date 16th March, 1846, Mr Gerard said:—'This wandering tuner has come back upon me and has taken my piano to pieces without asking leave. I had 9 bawbees, that is all! For mercy to a poor sinner give 60 bawbees, and charge me.' The tuner certified that he had received payment from Mr Allan as follows:—'Received the above (not in bawbees), but as good, say in silver, and a passage to Huna.—James Davie, jr.'

"Writing to a solicitor in Edinburgh in December, 1842, Mr Gerard incidentally gives a glimpse of his parish work. He says:—'I have many letters to write and answer every week. The duty of such a parish is more than mortal man can perform. The number of sick and distressed is very great. They value my quackery. If I shall refuse to prescribe they are directed to the best doctors in haste. I tell them plainly their danger. Thus they say if I do no good in such cases, they are confident

I shall do them no harm. All for nothing—no matter for some pounds spent in drugs—I get their blessing . . . My heart is warm as it was sixty years ago. Cut off sixty years and I am just entering my teens. I am coming into the region of feeling . . . I am feeling for an everlasting life in a clearer state of existence. All with whom I have lived are objects of my concern. What do I owe them? What neglect of duty to them? That atonement and compensation can I make where I may have wronged any of them? What are they now? Where shall I meet them, and what shall our future residence together be? . . . If you hear the roar of ridicule against the doctrine just ask these questions—Tell me the limits of the powers of darkness? Tell me the connection of the world of spirits with our souls?'

"In another letter to the same correspondent, Mr Gerard not only referred to his critics, but dealt with a suggestion which had been made to him to print some of his writings. He said:—'To the malignant and unfeeling critic my letters are the subject of bitter sarcasm, and are denounced as oddities—wild and extravagant effusions. There are reasons for this . . . I was twenty-five years of age when I finished at Marischall College and therefore ought to bring with me more than the giddy boy who began a short curriculum at thirteen. Now, I often hit off an idea suggested by something taught and remembered that few know or feel. This is the subject of sport to the ignorant, and would-be critic. My intimate acquaintance with my Bible from early days, and accurate study of theology, enable me to say some things that will never fail to please the person who has thought seriously for eternity. Some of my friends (perhaps flatterers) have advised me to publish some of my thoughts, and said they would sell. I have a peculiar horror to appearing in print, and therefore I have never said that I will do this. Perhaps I may venture a little bookie at a shilling, for the following reasons: I taught twenty-eight years in four parochial schools; I have been forty-two years a preacher, and that from sixty-five pulpits from Edinburgh to the ends of Orkney, and had the charge of two parishes twenty-eight years— Arbuthnot and this parish— and I preached almost constantly in Aberdeen thirteen years, where many thousands heard me in the different churches there. Thousands knew me, but I knew neither their names nor occupations. Now, many of all these might venture a shilling to see what I would say. Yea, if my age and infirmities and duties to my parish would permit me to extend my best thoughts, my posterity would have a kinder motive than curiosity for reading them, and the partiality of an old scholar, a well-wisher, and a parishioner, might be inclined to buy and read from a kind motive, too!'

"It will thus be seen," continued Watty, "that Mr Gerard knew quite well his sayings were much discussed and criticised. Writing to a correspondent three years before he died (in 1847), he said: 'I feel keenly, and express myself strongly. It is true that some have been pleased with these effusions, but colder writers have declared them extravagant nonsense.' Some people might think that his queer sayings were delivered on the spur of the moment, but I incline to the belief that Mr Gerard's ideas were the outcome of serious thought. It is well known to you all that when he had to deliver a funeral discourse, he was in the habit of writing, as a marginal note, opposite a pathetic passage where he wished to shed tears, the expressive words, 'Greet here!'

"Mr Gerard died in 1850," added Watty with a sigh, at the same time suspiciously blowing his nose and rubbing away the moisture which had gathered in the corners of his eyes. "I followed his remains to the North Churchyard, South Ronaldsay. The inscription on his tombstone is as follows:— 'In memory of Jane Craig, wife of Rev. John Gerard, who died 30th January, 1837; and of the Rev. John Gerard, minister of South Ronaldsay and Burray, who died 2nd October, 1850, in the 85th year of his age, the 45th year of his ministry, and the 36th of his incumbency.'

"Mr Gerard's son was educated for the ministry, but he only preached once or twice. He was offered his father's charge in 1850, but he declined the call."

When Watty concluded his narrative as given above, one of the younger members of the company suggested that he might relate some of the humorous anecdotes regarding Mr Gerard, which he was known to have collected from time to time.

"No, no," replied Watty. "The 'amers must be raked' now, but if we were to begin with these reminiscences it would be time to yoke tomorrow morning before we got through with them. However, if you care to come across to my house this night week, I will try and oblige you."

Taking this broad hint that it was time to go, the company separated, resolving, however, to accept the invitation so freely given by their old friend Watty Sinclair.

The news soon spread over the parish that Watty Sinclair was going to give reminiscences of Mr Gerard, with the result that nearly every family in the district was represented when we next gathered around his peat-fire. Watty had on his spectacles, which was the best token he could have given that he was in a good mood. After pipes had been filled, the weather discussed, and Mrs Sinclair's homebrewn ale had been sampled, Watty was invited to tell some stories regarding Mr Gerard.

"Well," said Watty, "as you all know, Mr Gerard was very quick in the temper, and as the habits and customs of the people then were very different from what they are now, he was often at variance with his parishioners. He was much annoyed with his neighbours' sheep and pigs roaming about the glebe. After giving due notice, he bought a gun and a mould for making leaden bullets, and shot several of the straying animals. This led to bad feeling on both sides, and Mr Gerard used to describe the owners of the offending animals as stupid brutes and devils! He once shot a pig and sent for the owner to come and take it away. Not knowing that the beast was dead, the owner asked Mr Gerard what he had to pay, and was blandly told there was no charge, because the pig had promised if it were taken away this time, it would never come back again!"

"Man," said Robbie Matches, "that puts me in mind of a story I have heard my father telling. A gentleman who was travelling through Orkney came to South Ronaldsay, and happening to call at the manse, he got such a kind reception that he remained for several days. He had the use of a horse to ride through the island, and a man to show him the sights in the various districts. One evening Mr Gerard asked his visitor to draw his chair up to the fire, as he was going to ask him a question. 'You have been travelling a good deal among my parishioners,' said Mr Gerard, 'and talking with them. Now, tell me honestly, do you think I am popular?' 'No,' replied the visitor. 'To tell you the truth, you are very unpopular.' 'Ah, I knew it,' retorted Mr Gerard; 'but did they tell you the reason why?' 'No.' 'Well, it is just because I am honest and tell them the truth. There is another parish that belongs to me besides this one. Pugh! I don't care a button for them—they are a set of poor ignorant creatures. I never preach a regular sermon there, but just take one of the commandments and moralise on it for a time. I have a good few half-sensible decent bodies in the North Parish, but some are very ignorant and unreasonable. The other Sabbath, as I was on my way to the South Kirk, I saw one of my neighbour's sheep in the identical park that I had forbidden them to enter, so I asked my man Willie to help me down off my pony, which he did. I then told him to catch the creature which he also did, when I took out my knife and cut its jugular vein, leaving it to bleed to death, that the people might see it as they went to the kirk.' "

"Did you ever hear what Mr Gerard said to the joiner about Mrs. Gerard when he was getting a little outhouse built?" asked old Mansie Budge, taking a hearty pinch of snuff, and quietly chuckling at the evident annoyance which his question had caused.

"Oh, yes," replied Watty Sinclair, "but you should understand that this is scarcely a fitting anecdote for the present occasion," giving a knowing look in the direction of the lasses, who were busily engaged at a spinning wheel outside the circle which surrounded the fire. "However, I will tell you a better story. You all know that if a girl is baptised in the same water after a boy she will be sure to sport whiskers before she dies. Well, Mr Gerard once told me something in this connection which is worth repeating. 'You know,' said he, 'that the inhabitants of the island over there (Burray?) are awfully prolific. They would have me dance over every now and then to baptise their bairns, but I let it be till it comes to the matter of ten or a dozen, and then do it all at once. The last time I was across, there was a large assembly of them in a barn. A table and a basin of water having been provided. A woman brought forward a bonnie wee mannie on his feet, and I baptised him and put them to their seats. I said to the next woman, 'bring forward your wean,' but she sat still. You should know that there is a midwife in the island named Lizzie Strachan, who has a motherly care over all the bairns she takes into the world. She came forward and said, 'You're no' gaun tae bapteeze this lassie oot o' the same water as the boy, or it'll be a living disgrace to her a' her life.' I answered— 'I am a minister of the Kirk of Scotland, come here to administer one of its most solemn ordinances, an' if ye dinna lat me bapteeze this lassie oot o' the same water, I'll bapteeze you, ye auld limmer that ye are. Without giving her time to answer, I threw the basin of water in her face, came down to the shore, and crossed over here. That is eighteen weeks ago and I haven't been there since'."

"Mr Gerard seems to have been very severe on the women," said Gilbert Tomison, as he for the first time took part in the discussion. "On one occasion there was a lady staying at the manse, and, as she was hospitably entertained, she appeared to be in no hurry to leave. One morning at breakfast Mr Gerard asked her if she read her Bible, to which she replied that she did. Mr Gerard then asked if she had read the 17th verse of the 25th chapter of Proverbs. Her reply was that she probably had but that she could not remember the words at that moment. 'Ah, well,' said Mr Gerard, 'you should read it now.' She apparently acted on her host's advice, for she took the hint and left the manse at once."

"Ah," said Mansie Budge, again breaking in upon the conversation, "Mr Gerard said some very queer things about women. Do you remember the kind of under-apparel he advised them to wear?"

"Man, Mansie," replied Watty Sinclair, "I wonder how it is that you can only recall what is nasty, and can never give us anything that's funny? As you all know, Mr Gerard was something of a poet. Well, he sent a piece of cloth to a tailor to get it made into a coat. The tailor was hard up for money, and yet he could not get time to make the garment. At last he sent asking Mr Gerard for an advance of a few shillings, when he received a reply in the following terms:—

'Lazy Johnnie Cumming, make my coat,
For I hae siller and thu has not;
Thu has my measure, and, as I said,
Mak' my coat and thu'll be paid'."

Robbie Duncan was now seen overhauling the contents of a large pocket-book. At last he produced a sheet of paper, yellow with age, which he reverently spread out on his knee. "Here," said he, "is a letter written by Mr Gerard. It seems that the bank agents at Kirkwall and Stromness had questioned the signature of Mr Gerard which appeared on a cheque tendered as payment for a debt. 'Manse of South Ronaldsay, 12th May, 1838.—Dear Sir,—Some fifty years ago the walls of the houses in Aberdeen were overlaid with large sheets with this inscription—'Wonders! Wonders!! Wonders!!! and wonders to be seen in the microscope of Dr Caterfelto.' Truly I add wonders! wonders!! wonders!!! and double wonders!!!! and one wonder more at the doubt of my much-loved friend J———— B———— about my writing my name . . .

It was upon the first of May,
I'll not forget th' eventful day,
I signed the bill with great good will,
And am your humble servant still,—
    John Gerard coarse,
    John Gerard fine,
    John Gerard with mine eyes dead shut'."

"I have as good a piece about Mr Gerard as that," said Jamie Cumming, anxious to contribute his share to the anecdotes. "Once Mr Gerard was invited to assist at the Communion services in St Magnus Cathedral, and the reply he sent was as follows:—

'I joy'd when to the House of God,
    Go up they said to me,
And soon within St Magnus' pile,
    Gerard shall standing be'."

"As you all know," resumed old Watty Sinclair, rubbing his spectacles, "in former times there was very little opportunity of advertising meetings in country districts. On one occasion the Rev. Walter Weir, who was then minister of Walls, was to preach at South Ronaldsay, and Mr Gerard was anxious that his parishioners should know this. He hit upon a novel expedient for advertising the fact. On the day before the sermon was to be delivered, he entered the parish school with his quick shuffling gait, and without once lifting his head to look at either master or pupils, walked right up to the desk. Here he gravely took off his hat and shouted—

'Sound the trumpet, blow the horn,
Walter Weir's to preach the morn.'

Without another word he marched out of the school as he had entered it. As might have been expected, an intimation made in this sensational manner soon spread over the whole parish, and Mr Gerard accomplished his object."

"Here's a story," said Mansie Budge, "which you will surely not object to. When Mr Gerard was in the middle of his discourse one day in his own church, two dogs fell a-fighting. The beadle rose to put them out, but Mr Gerard, who was an interested spectator, shouted, to the amusement of the congregation—

'Let them alane, Tammas, let them alane.
I'll wager ye twopence the brown ane will gain!' "

"Aye, that's a better one," was Watty Sinclair's comment upon it. Continuing, he said—"One day Mr Gerard came up to my father with a long face and said, 'Watty, there is a ghost up at the manse!' My father expressed doubts on the matter. 'Well,' said Mr Gerard, 'when my wife went into the meal girnal today she found a ghost. There was nothing in it!' Mr Gerard liked this joke so well that he repeated it to the factor at Graemeshall—writing to that gentleman in similar terms to let him know that he required a supply of oatmeal."

"Sometimes at meetings of his session," said Robbie

Matches, "Mr Gerard lost his temper, as I suppose you have all heard, and on these occasions he made things pretty hot for those who tried to thwart him. At the close of a heated discussion in the session one night an elder put on his long silk hat to leave the meeting. This gave so much offence to Mr Gerard that he took hold of the hat, pulled it down over the offending elder's nose and kept the brim of the ruined head-gear as a memento of the scuffle. You may rely on the truth of that story, for my father, who saw it, told me all about it."

Meantime Watty Sinclair was engaged hunting through a drawer of the dresser, and when he returned to the fireside he had with him a bundle of papers, neatly rolled up, and carefully fastened with a cord. Slowly opening the roll, Watty said, "A parishioner got into trouble once for doing a little smuggling, and on asking for a certificate from Mr Gerard to give to the Justices who were to try him, he received a letter in the following terms, dated 'Manse of South Ronaldsay, May 21, 1846:—The bearer Donald Symison, aged 66, has been my near neighbour these thirty-one years—quietly and soberly an example to any farmer in my widespread parish. I am grieved that his fine feeling of generosity to his thirsty kind neighbours in the yearly day of joy in cutting his peats tempted him to make a little malt! He bids me say for him that he is a poor man, and not fit to stand any operation. I join in his desire, and confidently hope that his honourable judges will cut off neither leg nor finger, and that he shall return to us sound in life and limb.—So hopes and prays John Gerard, minister'."

"That shows that Mr Gerard's heart was in the right place," said Mansie Budge, "and I will now give you another instance of the same kind. As you all know, he was very severe on drunkards. Well, one of the members of his congregation had been before the Session several times for this offence, and at last Mr Gerard lost all patience with him. He got into a passion, and what do you think he likened a drunkard to?"

"Come, come, Mansie," cried Watty excitedly, "that's not a fit story for the present company. You can keep that one till the first time you are down at the public house in the Hope, and you will then have a suitable audience."

Watty Sinclair seemed very angry at Mansie Budge for having alluded to the anecdote regarding the drunkard; but after getting a friendly pinch of snuff from Robbie Matches' mull he was persuaded to give another story. He said— "Preaching in his own church one day on the rich man and Lazarus, Mr Gerard gravely told his hearers that there was plenty of evidence in the Bible that the rich man had been buried"; but, he added, "the same cannot be said of poor Lazarus. The fact is, I believe the unfortunate fellow was eaten up, rump and stump, by the dogs that caught the crumbs which fell from the table of the rich man!"

"On another occasion," said Gilbert Tomison, "Mr Gerard was holding forth on the text: 'Thou shalt love thy neighbour as thyself.' He said it was not always easy to obey a commandment of that kind. For instance, how could he be expected to be on good terms with the laird of——, seeing that gentleman had come up to the manse six months ago for a 'caisie,' which he had not yet returned. The laird referred to took this broad hint, and returned the article next day."

"Mr Gerard was grand in prayer," said Watty Sinclair. "Well, when the late James Craig was rector of the Kirkwall Grammar School, Mr Gerard paid that institution a visit, and after examining the children on religious knowledge, engaged in prayer, in which he put up the following petition:—'We pray thee, O Lord, that Thy grace may stick to the hearts of Craig's boys like butter to bere bannocks!' I can assure you that no scholar who heard that prayer ever forgot it."

"I tell you what it is, lads," declared Mansie Budge, "I don't deny that Mr Gerard was capital at prayer, but I know he was also a very keen sportsman. He was asked to preach at Orphir at a Sacramental preparatory service. When crossing from South Ronaldsay his boat got becalmed, and it was past the hour of meeting before the minister hove in sight. That no time might be lost, the office-bearers resolved that they should proceed with the introductory services themselves, so that the preacher would be able to commence his sermon immediately on his arrival. Even when the prayer, praise, and reading lesson were over, however, Mr Gerard had not put in an appearance

so two of the elders went out to ascertain the cause of the
delay. As they proceeded along the burn which ran down past
the church towards the sea, they saw a man stripped to the
trousers, plunging out and in the water in the most ludicrous
fashion. But when they got nearer, and found Mr Gerard
divested of boots, stockings, coat, vest and hat, they were
considerably astonished. They explained that the congregation
had been waiting his arrival for nearly an hour. 'Oh, it's all
right,' was Mr Gerard's reply. 'I saw a nest of wild ducks in the
burn, and I thought it would be a pity to let them escape. I
have seven of them in my hat, but there's one little deevil here
yet, which I must catch before I go up to the church.' And he
did get it, before he was prevailed upon to go and preach his
sermon!"

"Aye, that's better," was Watty Sinclair's complimentary
comment on the above. "That reminds me of a story regarding
Mr Gerard and the Orphir Kirk. Our old minister was

preaching there on a Sacramental occasion—it was on a Monday, the day of thanksgiving. Dogs, some of them very decent brutes, had not then given up the habit of attending kirk, and a little band of curs had found a seat on the stone-paved passage which ran up through the middle of the building. During the sermon a snarling was heard, and still louder snarling. Mr Gerard at last lost all patience and looking down to the beadle said—'John, pray, do put out these dogs. I cannot get on, they make such a din.' Mr Gerard sat down, and the people, some of them not very devout, waited with amusement till the profane dogs were dismissed. In a similar case, but in a different parish, the following is said to have taken place. The beadle-policeman sternly eyeing an intruder dog, addressed him thus—'Come oot here, ye lang, hungry scoonral, ye dinna belang to oor congregation ava!' "

"I need not tell you," said Mansie Budge, "that Mr Gerard had a mechanical turn of mind, but his saw got so blunt he could not use it. He therefore took it to a joiner to get it sharpened. The tradesman did the job to Mr Gerard's entire satisfaction, but he absolutely refused to take any payment for the work. 'Weel, weel,' said Mr Gerard to the joiner, 'you are a young man, and who knows but you may yet have to stand before the session, and if you have the good fortune to come before mine, I will remember the sharpening of the saw!' "

"Ah, he was a wonderful man, was Mr Gerard," replied Robbie Matches. "He was of a most generous disposition. No beggar was ever turned away from his door, and I have heard it said of him that he was so ready in assisting his more needy neighbours, that he often crippled himself. One day he met two strangers near his manse, and on ascertaining that they came from a neighbouring island, he said he was sure they were sadly in need of refreshment. After a little conversation he invited them to his house to enjoy his hospitality. When the tea was put on the table Mr Gerard thus addressed his guests:—'Now, my men, I know that you must be hungry after such a long journey, so you can be spreading the butter on your bread whilst I am asking a blessing, and that will save time!' "

"What I liked best about Mr Gerard," said Watty Sinclair "was his ready tongue. On one occasion he had to attend a meeting of Presbytery at Kirkwall for the purpose of hearing the trials of a young probationer under call. Though a snowstorm was raging, the members of Presbytery were certain that Mr Gerard would attend, and they resolved to await his arrival. Occasionally messengers were sent out to have a look in the direction of the Holm Road, in the hope of descrying their absent brother. At length the probationer took his turn, and when he came back reported that he saw someone coming along the road with his head wrapped up in shawls, and bestriding an old horse, which reminded him of nothing so much as Balaam and his ass. This was duly reported to Mr Gerard when he arrived at the Cathedral, but to the surprise of all present he paid no attention to the offending probationer. Subsequently, however, when the young minister flourished a large number of testimonials in the face of the Presbytery, and these were passed along to Mr Gerard, that gentleman flung them from him with the remark—'Tak' them awa'. We all know that dirty bairns require many cloths!' "

"Mr Gerard was a plain body himself," said Robbie Matches, "and could not stand anything that was uppish, such as a big display of starched linen. Well, amongst the candidates for the Firth Kirk at one time was a masher student, who spoke with a strong Cockney twang, though he had probably never been nearer London than myself. One day this young masher met Mr Gerard and asked him what his chance was of getting the presentation. Mr Gerard pointed to a tree and a pig in the vicinity. 'Do you see these?' asked Mr Gerard. 'Yes,' was the reply. 'Well, there is as much chance of that pig climbing up that tree tail foremost, and whistling 'Maggie Lauder,' as there is of you becoming minister of the Parish Kirk of Firth!' "

"That story," said Mansie Budge, "reminds me of a discussion that Mr Gerard had with the Presbytery, as to whether anything could be nasty and yet not sinful. Do you remember how Mr Gerard proved that some things could be nasty and not sinful?"

"Tuts, tuts," replied Watty Sinclair, "it's queer that you

always want to discuss that class of stories: but I'll not have that one told in my house."

Mansie thereupon collapsed, and Robbie Matches took advantage of the lull in the conversation to continue—"Mr Gerard was one day preaching to his own congregation on charity, and told them that they grudged to drop a penny in the plate for the poor, or give a sixpence to the Lord, but that they would go away down to the Hope and give a dirty drunken old Highland piper there a shilling to play that abominable tune, 'He's Ower the Hills and Far Awa'!'—illustrating the remark by walking round the pulpit pretending he was playing the bagpipes."

"Aye, Mr Gerard was indeed very queer in the pulpit," said Mansie Budge. "I suppose you all remember the time when his son preached two Sabbaths in succession from the same text, and what a surprise we got on the third Sunday when Mr Gerard announced the very same words for his discourse. His introduction explained everything, however. He said he wanted to clear away the fog that Johnnie had thrown around the text, and to explain that youth's babblings. It was an awful thing for a father to do to a son, and it ended the ministerial career of the latter. "But," continued Mansie, "our old minster said some very sly things. When the Rev. Andrew White came to be U.P. minister here, he caused quite a flutter amongst the ladies of his congregation. He was unmarried, and got many presents from them. Mr Gerard hearing of this, said—'Well, if the Lord was only half as fond of me as the lasses are of Andrew White, I would not be long here'."

"I remember that fine," said Watty Sinclair, "and it gave us all a hearty laugh. You all know," continued Watty, "that Mr Gerard had no sympathy with the Disruption movement. Well, just before the Disruption in 1843, an old college companion wrote him asking him if he intended leaving the Establishment. 'Do you think,' replied Mr Gerard, 'that I am such a stupid as to come out, after all the trouble I had to get in?' "

"Our old minister had quite as little sympathy with the Voluntary movement," said Robbie Matches, "I remember hearing that the late Mr McGuffie, the first U.P. minister located in South Ronaldsay, gave Mr Gerard the loan of an expensive book on the Voluntary controversy, and when it was returned to him he was considerably annoyed to find that it had been freely marked along the margin of the leaves. He therefore wrote a sharp note of complaint to Mr Gerard, when he received the following quaint reply:—'Dost thou well to be angry, Peter.—J. Gerard!' "

"That," continued Robbie, "reminds me of another story which I may give you when I am at it. The Rev. Mr Miller, who succeeded the Rev. Mr McGuffie just referred to, announced on one occasion that he intended to preach in the schoolhouse on a certain day. Mr Gerard hearing of this, and thinking he ought to have been consulted before the parish school was used for such a purpose, advertised a meeting for the same hour and place. He was a little late in arriving, and by that time Mr Miller had commenced the service. When he entered the room, however, Mr Miller at once intimated that he hoped Mr Gerard would continue the service, and forthwith left the desk. Mr Gerard had gone to the school-house prepared to stick up for what he considered his rights, but, appreciating the kindly spirit of his opponent, and not to be outdone in a display of courtesy, he insisted that Mr Miller, being the younger man, should deliver the sermon. This arrangement was ultimately agreed to, and after the service Mr Miller dined with Mr Gerard at the manse, and thus commenced a friendship that was only broken by death."

"Look here, lads," said Mansie Budge, "I think I must tell you what Mr Gerard considered the best qualities for a wife. When he used to visit Kirkwall, nothing pleased him so much as to meet with a few young men who were studying music, for the purpose of hearing them sing. Addressing his musical class one night, he said he supposed they would all be on the look-out for a wife, and he therefore gave them directions for securing a suitable one. The great qualities to be looked for in a good wife all commenced with a 'p' and were five in number. The first was the personage. He was sure none of them would care to marry an old hag as ugly as sin! The next quality was parentage. They should look out for a woman

with respectable parents, for few people would like to marry
the daughter of a hangman! He coupled the next two qualities
together, which were piety and prudence. These two graces
did not always go together, for a young woman might be pious
and lack prudence. He once heard of a young man who had
the chance of a wife who was pious but not prudent, and
another who was prudent but not pious. The poor fellow
found it so difficult to decide which was the better, he sought
the advice of his minister on the matter, who counselled him
to take the prudent wife. The young man, however, preferred
the pious one, and shortly after the marriage he confessed to
the minister that he had made a mistake, for her piety had
been scattered to the four winds of heaven, and she had turned
out a regular Tartarean! Mr Gerard's own advice was that if
the choice lay between piety and prudence, the latter should
be preferred. The last quality he would advise them to look
for was patrimony. This was not absolutely indispensable for
their happiness in married life, but they would find it to be
far more enjoyable than poverty."

"As you remember," interrupted Watty Sinclair, "our
minister was sometimes peculiar in his manner to visitors. The
two sons of a Free Church minister went to stay with Mr
Gerard shortly after the Disruption. Their father had been an
intimate acquaintance of Mr Gerard's prior to 1843, so that
they were very heartily entertained whilst they were residing
at the South Ronaldsay Manse. When they were about to leave
they were very effusive in their thanks, and their host did not
like this. Getting them outside the door, he said—'Gang awa'
hame, ye perjured villains. Ye cam' here to get some fun oot
o' old Gerard, but I'm thinking he has got ye ootside noo an'
he'll keep ye there!' "

"I have heard my father saying," said Robbie Matches,
"that on one occasion Mr Gerard, when returning from the
General Assembly, took the overland route. When he arrived
at Wick, he called upon the parish minister there, a Mr Phin.
He was told that Mr Phin was engaged and could not see him.
Mr Gerard was not to be put off in this fashion, and said he
would wait the convenience of Mr Phin. He was ushered into
a dirty, poorly-furnished apartment and was kept waiting

there for a long time. When at last Mr Phin made his appearance, there was nothing in the garb of the visitor to indicate that he was a minister, and he treated Mr Gerard with some gruffness for having disturbed him. Mr Gerard then opened out on the Wick parson, by asking him why he put his visitors into a scullery, meanly furnished with an old black painted chair, and a broken-down three-legged table. He gave it as his opinion that no minister of the Established Church should treat people in such a fashion. 'Why, for anything you knew,' added Mr Gerard, 'I might have been one of your own parishioners wanting you to go and minister to a dying friend, but before you could have got to him the breath would probably have been out of him.' 'And who is it that dares use such language to me?' pompously asked the Wick minister. 'It is your neighbour minister from South Ronaldsay,' was the prompt reply. Mr Gerard's fame had, of course, spread to Herringopolis, and he was at once invited upstairs to partake of the hospitality of the manse. The invitation, however, was not accepted; but the Rev. Mr Phin laid to heart the advice given him and is said to have treated his visitors in a very different manner ever after."

"I will now tell you the only other story I know about Mr Gerard," said Mansie Budge, as he began to fill his pipe. "A parishioner called on our minister one day and informed him that some person had entered his barn and had stolen a quantity of his corn. At that time ministers were credited with powers which they never claimed to possess, and Mr Gerard was not at all surprised when he was requested to find out the thief. He promised he would do it. On the following Sabbath, in the course of his intimations, in which he expatiated on all the gossip of the previous week, he intimated to his congregation that John————of———— house had had some corn taken out of his barn on such and such a day, that the thief was in the church, and that if he did not immediately rise, take up his hat, and walk out of the building, he would expose him before the whole congregation! The culprit was so much taken by surprise by the suddenness of the accusation, and was so frightened at the threat, that he actually obeyed the order, and walked out of the church!"

"Well, lads," said Watty Sinclair, "I commenced these yarns tonight, and I will finish them. I have heard it said that when the first United Presbyterian Church was in course of erection in South Ronaldsay, and before the roof was got on, a terrific storm arose which blew down one of the gables of the building. Upon this news being communicated to Mr Gerard next day, he remarked—'The deil and I used to pull on opposite ends of the rope, but it seems that we have been pulling together last night!' Our old minister," added Watty, "could not help saying those queer things; but he was a faithful pastor and a loving and steadfast friend. May it be ours to imitate what was best in his character, and may we all die loved and respected as he was."

As Watty concluded, there was a tremor in his voice that gave evidence of how keen his feelings were on the loss of his old pastor; and when the party broke up, the "Good-nights" were subdued, showing that the company, including Mansie Budge, were all in sympathy with him.

CHARLES W. HEDDLE

Some winters ago, a number of merchants and travellers were storm-stayed at Sanday. They had taken up their quarters at the hotel near the pier. The snow was falling so thickly that it was out of the question to attempt work. Everything outside was as bleak as could be imagined. The sea could be heard dashing in upon the shore, but it could not be seen. The windows were so frosted and bespattered with snow, as to act as an effectual blind, so that land and ocean were hidden from view.

But inside they were perfectly happy. They had a blazing fire, and several members of the company possessed a large store of anecdotes of all kinds. After studying the visitors' book, they began to talk of eminent Orcadians, such as Dr Baikie, the African traveller; Dr Leask, the theologian; David Vedder, the poet; and Samuel Laing, the financier and politician.

A Kirkwall Town Councillor, who had hitherto taken no part in the discussion, at length said he would tell a story which was not generally known, regarding an Orcadian millionaire.

"I suppose," said he, "that you have all heard of Charles W. Heddle, the merchant prince; but I am sure none of you know that by a will dated November 27, 1888, he left the residue of his estate to the town of Kirkwall, which was estimated to amount to nearly half a million sterling.

"Mr Heddle came from a remarkable stock on the paternal side. His grandfather, Mr John Heddle, was in 1788 appointed Town Clerk of Kirkwall, an office which he held for a long period. Nineteen years previously, when quite a young man, he had set up business in the Burgh as a lawyer, and in that capacity fought and won a great battle for the working classes.

"At that time the Kirkwall Magistrates forced tradesmen to leave their work and act as soldiers on special occasions, such as the great Lammas Fair. In the year 1769, the Municipal authorities, who were all wealthy traders, called out the Lammas Guard to clear the streets of stranger merchants, because they considered that these people, by underselling them, were destroying their business.

"The working classes looked upon this move as oppressive, and some of the guard refused to act. There were promptly apprehended and put into prison. Mr John Heddle took up their case, carried it to the Court of Session, and succeeded in freeing the people from such military services in all time coming.

"During this conflict the Magistrates showed great hostility to Mr Heddle and described him as the son of a tradesman, who had come as a firebrand in their midst to stir up strife and trouble. However, his ability was so conspicuous that the Magistrates, nineteen years later, appointed him Town Clerk of the Burgh.

"Dr John Heddle, a son of the Town Clerk, and father of the subject of my narrative, was a very distinguished officer, was Inspector-General of Fleets and Hospitals in his day, and captured Goree and Senegal from the French almost single-handed.

"Charles W. Heddle, the son of the last-named gentleman, though born in West Africa, was sent home to be educated, first at Kirkwall, and subsequently at Edinburgh Academy. Some old people still alive remember him quite well. He had all the pluck of both his father and his grandfather, and was the hero of many a schoolboy fight. With his companions he was a great favourite owing to the daring which he showed under all circumstances. His favourite amusement was to sail boats in the Peerie Sea, and he was so successful in getting out to the holm there before his companions that he was dubbed the 'Prince of the Holmie'—(Prince of Dahomey).

"Having inherited some money from his father, and getting an advance from Mr Robert Heddle, he proceeded to Sierra Leone. When there he partly made a new trade, and partly picked up the threads of one from which his uncle, Mr Robert Heddle, had retired.

"Charles Heddle might be described as half a native of Africa, so that he was well able to stand the climate, and he made money very rapidly. His uncle, whilst in Africa, had accumulated a sum of £90,000; but Charles was able to remain out much longer, and when he retired his fortune was probably little less than a million sterling.

"People going out to Africa from Orkney were always warmly welcomed and generously assisted by Charles Heddle; but unfortunately most of them were unable to stand the climate (though Sierra Leone itself is now comparatively healthy), and usually either died or had to come home exhausted by malarial fever.

"In passing, I may mention that it was in Charles Heddle's house at Sierra Leone that Dr Baikie, the African traveller, died on 12th December, 1864, he having taken coast fever on coming down from the healthy country far up the Niger. As showing the adventurous spirit of Orcadians, it is also worth recalling that Charles Heddle, a brother of Mr J. G. Moodie-Heddle of Melsetter, when being sent home from Africa ill of fever some years ago, died on board ship at Cape de Verde Islands, just as another brother, Robert Heddle, passed outward bound to New Zealand.

"When Charles Heddle retired from business he found that he was unable to stand the London fog, or the cold further north, so that he went to live in France, where he purchased a palatial residence. Whilst there, he made a will in which quite a number of bequests were set forth, and the deed concluded—'If my aforesaid adopted son, John Francis Caille Heddle, should die without lawful issue, I bequeath the residue of my estate in trust to the Provost and Magistrates of the Burgh of Kirkwall, in the County of Orkney, Scotland, for the time being, to be applied and expended to the improvement and better endowment of the existing charitable and educational institutions of the said Burgh of Kirkwall, or in the erection and endowment of such others as may be deemed and considered needful and necessary.'

"That will, as I have already stated, was dated 27th November, 1888, but some time subsequently Mr Heddle made the acquaintance of a French-Canadian lady, whom he married. Regarding this lady very little is known, but she is represented as having been only about twenty-three years of age, whilst her husband was a man of between seventy and eighty. After this marriage a new will was made, by which most of the fortune was transferred to the young wife, and a small sum was left to the 'adopted son,' John F. C. Heddle.

"Shortly afterwards Charles Heddle died, and it is said that the widow presented the 'adopted son' with £120,000.

"Some of the beneficiaries under the 1888 will contested the deed in favour of the widow, in the French courts, but were unsuccessful.

"The Magistrates of Kirkwall employed a London lawyer to watch the case on their behalf while it was being tried in France, but as their interest in the will only became active in the event of John F. C. Heddle dying without issue, they did not really become parties to the suit.

"The upshot of the trial was a great disappointment to the Town Council of Kirkwall, for the interest on the residue of the estate would not only have been sufficient to have paid off all the debt of the Burgh, but would have freed the residents from taxes in all time coming."

When the Town Councillor concluded his narrative, a Kirkwall merchant, who formed one of the company, laid aside his pipe, at which he had been vigorously puffing, and said he would give the story of Sandy Burgess.

SANDY BURGESS

"From a merchant prince to poor Sandy Burgess, one of the characters of Kirkwall," he continued, "is a big leap. The one died in affluence, the other in abject poverty, but the pauper will probably be remembered by the inhabitants of Kirkwall long after the other is forgotten.

"Early in the present century, the father of Sandy Burgess, who was then a member of the Ninth Royal Veteran Battalion, was located in Kirkwall for some time, and after he was pensioned off he returned here, got married, and settled down in the place.

"Sandy Burgess was one of the children of the marriage. When he left school he was apprenticed to a tailor, but he could not settle down to the bench. He had a great love for horses and when quite a young lad he could make the boast that there was not an animal in Orkney that could throw him.

"Probably his best days were when he acted as groom or stableman at Berstane for the late Mr William Balfour, and at that time he was a regular dandy. He could sport a yellow waistcoat, long hat, and a very stylishly-cut coat. Got up in this rig, he used to cause quite a flutter in the United Presbyterian Church on Sundays as he entered it.

"Sandy was possessed of a pretty crop of curly hair, of which he was justly proud, and nothing pleased him so much as to be flattered regarding it. When he left his situation at Berstane, he went about idle for some time, till the then proprietor of *The Orcadian* newspaper found some employment for him. For a year or two Sandy helped to ink *The Orcadian* every week, filling in his odd time by doing clerical work—he being a good penman.

"He could never be taught, however, that a newspaper, to be of any value, had to be issued with clock-like regularity. If, for instance, the Queen's Birthday and the day of publication came on together, Sandy's loyalty to Her Majesty was too strong to allow him to work at the paper, and he might be depended upon to make his appearance in the printing office, with long hat and yellow waistcoat, smelling badly of rum—

which, by the way, was his favourite drink. This was his usual mode of indicating that he had struck work, and neither persuasion nor threats had any effect upon him under such circumstances. The paper might be published fifty-two times in the year, but Her Majesty's Birthday could only be celebrated once annually, and Sandy therefore gave himself up to drinking rum and singing comic songs for twelve hours at least.

"In August, 1856, the Prince of Orange visited Orkney. That was a great day for Sandy. Dressed up in a borrowed suit, and with his long curls fluttering in the breeze he looked a perfect masher. The cause of his get-up was that he had been fixed upon as the jehu that should drive His Royal Highness out to the Standing Stones of Stenness.

"When the supreme moment arrived for starting, Sandy handled the whip with such science as to call forth a tremendous cheer from the crowd, for the people were really delighted that he had been selected for the honour. The Prince, innocently thinking that he was the object of the ovation, bowed his acknowledgements which greatly added to the hilarity of the onlookers.

"In after years if Sandy heard anyone praising the horsemanship of an opponent, his usual reply was— 'Aye, he may be a very great man, but who drove the Prince of Orange when he was in Orkney?' And the withering look which generally accompanied this question was amply sufficient to silence anyone who tried to slight Sandy by making unfavourable contrasts.

"With the children he was a great favourite. Nothing pleased him better than to have a band of youngsters round him singing songs to them. 'Any Old Shoes to Mend' was his masterpiece, and he could do it so well that he actually carried off a prize by rendering it at a public competition.

"He was a splendid mimic. He was in the habit of imitating an old woman at her spinning-wheel with such realism that it was worth going a journey to witness the performance. Pretending he was turning a wheel he would sit crooning an old Orkney air, and all at once would stop, order the cat out of the way, chastise it for meddling with the wool, just as an old woman might be supposed to do, and then catch up the refrain at the exact bar where he was supposed to have been interrupted. The whole thing was so naturally done, and the asides which he indulged in were really so humorous, that those who have witnessed the performance will not soon forget it.

"Sandy's great failing was, as I have already indicated, a love of rum, and, when he was employed as a driver, he had to be closely watched. He had an immense store of old-world anecdotes, and there was scarcely a farmhouse which he passed which did not recall some interesting story or another to his mind. It therefore naturally followed that before his destination was reached, he succeeded in making such a favourable impression upon his employers that he would probably be rewarded with a handsome tip to get refreshments for himself whilst he was waiting for the return journey. Under such circumstances he invariably went to the bad. When the travellers were ready to start it was generally difficult to find Sandy; or, if he was got, more than likely he would have a crowd of children round him delighting them with a comic song, such as 'Tillie-Tillie-Arum,' or 'The Nice Little Town that We Live In,' and he himself so far gone in drink that he would be unable to manage the horse that was under his charge.

"Notwithstanding Sandy's delinquencies in this respect, however, he was rarely reported for misconduct; indeed, he was rather in demand than otherwise, and it was only when overtaken by old age that he left his situation as driver.

"In his latter years he picked up a precarious living by making himself generally useful about the Castle Hotel, brushing boots, plucking hens, and running messages. This is the sort of work he was performing when the fourth centenary of the erection of Kirkwall into a royal burgh was celebrated. Sandy, who was dressed up in all the grandeur which had distinguished him in former years, took part in the procession of trades, riding on a pony, and carrying in his arms a large turkey, which was intended to intimate to all and sundry that he was the hen-plucker for the burgh. The fowl was alive and did not appreciate the honour done to it. Sandy, in acknowledging the cheers of the populace, let loose his hold on its neck, and his nose carried the marks of the turkey's bill for many a day afterwards.

"As long as Mrs Ross remained in the Castle Hotel, Sandy had a good friend, who took care that he was fed and kept in clothing. When she left the place, however, he became ill-off. He was one of those quiet, harmless, inoffensive creatures who would rather starve than tell that he was needful, and he was never known to beg. In his latter days he seemed to shun the public gaze, and it must be confessed that he was somewhat neglected. On 8th June, 1888, he was found lying in a stable at Castle Street, apparently in a dying condition. Though the hour was late, the Inspector of Poor was communicated with, and poor Sandy was conveyed to the poorhouse that same night. He gradually sank, and on the 20th of the same month he breathed his last. His age, I believe, was about sixty-five years."

A tall, slender farmer, who had been an interested listener to the two previous sketches, volunteered to give the story of George Taylor.

GEORGE TAYLOR

"George Taylor," said he, "was a poor Kirkwall boy, who rose from the lowest rung in the ladder to one of the very highest positions in the British Army. The story of his life, you will all agree with me, reads like a romance. He started his career as a message boy to Mr Urquhart, tailor, Kirkwall, about the end of the eighteenth century.

"The Urquharts were well known in their day, though there is not one of the family now remaining in Kirkwall. The great John Urquhart was a man who stood 6 feet 3 inches in his stocking soles, and he was the first to cut English cloth in the capital of Orkney. But he had an untimely end. In trying to protect Mr Shireff, the then Sheriff-Substitute of Orkney, during an election riot, in 1832, he was butted so severely on the back that he died three days afterwards.

"Evidently George Taylor did not find the work here to his taste, for he left Mr Urquhart's employment and proceeded to Melsetter, where he was engaged as a clerk in the estate office. Whilst there his penmanship attracted the attention of Dr Barry, the author of the *History of Orkney*. Dr Barry's calligraphy was bad, and that gentleman asked young Taylor to copy out his work, and to make it ready for the printer, a request which was gladly complied with.

"When the book was finished, Dr Barry submitted the M.S. to Sir John Sinclair of Ulbster, to get his opinion of the work. The beautiful writing was much admired by Sir John (who happened to be on board a man-of-war vessel which was then lying at Longhope). Sir John asked to see young Taylor, and was so much impressed by his appearance that he offered him a commission in the Caithness and Ross-shire Fencibles, which was at once accepted.

"Four years later, George Taylor had saved a little money and he bought a commission in the ranks, the sum paid being £400. He passed his examination with such credit that he was advanced from ensign to lieutenant, and was told that if he would raise a company of twenty-six men in his native county he would be gazetted as a captain.

"Thereupon he went to Kirkwall and succeeded in getting fourteen men to join the ranks, and at Longhope, and in other districts in Orkney, he soon secured the additional number of recruits.

"He was then made a captain in the 29th Regiment, where he became a great favourite with the Colonel, Sir Francis Wilder. About this time the young captain fell in love with a Miss Phillip, who was a sister of the Colonel's wife.

"As Miss Phillip was a wealthy young lady, and as George Taylor was poor, the lovers seemed to have their doubts as to whether her father would agree to the match. They accordingly got married without consulting the bride's father; but next day they waited upon him and told him what they had done. To their surprise he expressed himself as quite satisfied with the match, and made a handsome settlement upon the daughter.

"Subsequently Taylor was sent out to Canada, where he had several brilliant engagements with the French, in one of which he was severely wounded in the thigh. Whilst there he bought a large estate.

"There were three children of this marriage—one son and two daughters. The son was educated for the ministry, but died at an early age, before he got an appointment. One of the daughters lived till about middle age, whilst the third reached nearly three score and ten before she died. This one married a Frenchman, and visited Orkney twice with her husband for the purpose of seeing her cousins—Mr Francis Taylor, at one time tenant of Howe, and his sister, Miss Taylor.

This lady got the half of the Canadian estate already referred to, and when she died a few years ago, she left it to Mr Francis Taylor and his sister. Mr F. Taylor bequeathed a sum of £1000 for the upkeep and repair of St Magnus Cathedral.

"I have seen a picture of George Taylor, taken about the time that he was married. He was then a young man of prepossessing appearance, more like a poet than a warrior, and reminded me very much of Lord Byron."

"Very good," was the approving comment of the company, which so pleased the farmer that he said he would now give the story of William and James Cumming.

WILLIAM AND JAMES CUMMING

"The subjects of this sketch," said he, "were brothers, and the present occupants of Sebay have descended from the same family. They were both educated at the Kirkwall Grammar School, and at that time lived at Grainbank, but subsequently their parents removed to Lingro.

"The boys being clever, and residing on the Graemeshall estate, it was quite natural that Admiral Graeme should take a fancy to them. William, who was a splendid linguist, when quite a young man, became connected with an important wine firm in London, and was sent all over the Continent to buy for the house.

"He happened to be in Spain or Portugal during the Peninsular War, and in the course of his travels rendered important services to the commissariat department of the British Army. Some officers had been sent out to gather stores, but they were so badly up in the language that the natives could not make out what they wanted. When in this dilemma, young Cumming came on the scene, and helped the officers to make their purchases.

"These gentlemen were so well pleased with his services that they insisted he should return with them to headquarters, where he was introduced to the Iron Duke. Up to this time the working of the commissariat department had been giving Wellington much anxiety, and when he saw that William Cumming was thoroughly conversant with the language of the people, he urged him to accept the management of that branch of the service.

"After a little persuasion Cumming took up the work, and he performed it so satisfactorily that he became a favourite with the Duke, and was handsomely rewarded after the war was over. Indeed, when he returned to London, he had the honour of being presented to the Royal Family.

"Afterwards he married a young lady belonging to the North of England, who had a fortune of £30,000 a year.

"The other brother was, by the influence of Admiral Graeme, appointed a purser in the Navy. During one of the many encounters which took place about that period between the British Fleet and that of France, James Cumming had the misfortune to be captured by the enemy. He was conveyed to France, and was kept in prison there for seven years. He once made an attempt to escape, which ended in failure. The fact is, that in jumping from the walls of the jail, he fell and broke his leg.

"After the war was over, he was set at liberty and rejoined the Navy. Subsequently he bought Quanterness and built a residence there, but he entered the house too soon after it was finished and he was found dead in bed next morning.

"His heir, Major Cumming, is still alive, and owns Quanterness."

The late Mr Duncan MacLean, who left Kirkwall in boyhood, in course of time joined the Navy, and for years led a thrilling life of adventure, finishing up as editor of the *Boston Traveller,* shortly before he died furnished us with the following particulars regarding the Cumming family:—

"In your sketch of this family you did not say anything about the third brother, and although I was cow-boy in the family myself about a year, I have forgotten his name, if I ever knew it. He, too, had the 'open sight,' and it was said that it was a ghostly vision which made him insane. Personally he was a picture of manly grandeur; stood over six feet high, broad shouldered, dark complexioned, and eyes that seemed to blaze with intellectual light. His constant companion was a white bulldog, which had been given to him by his brother, the purser. When the 'dark spirit' was upon him, he walked backwards and forwards in a small paved yard near the house, playing the most dismal sounds upon the bagpipes. His two maiden sisters managed the farm, and managed it well, also taking care of him. Sometimes I tried to approach him, but without speaking a word he scowled me from him; I never heard him utter a word to anyone. I saw his brother, the purser, who had served in the Navy, and I remember that he left a copy of 'Falconer's Shipwreck,' which I read with wonder and delight. This family has also passed away."

"That reminds me," said the Town Councillor, "of the story of a Kirkwall boy, named Robert Smith.

ROBERT SMITH

"About the close of the last, or beginning of the present century, some vessels belonging to the British Fleet anchored in Kirkwall bay, and a number of the officers came ashore, expressing a desire to go out and see the Standing Stones of Stenness.

"There were no carriages in Orkney in those days, but the tenant of Lingro had a drove of Shetland ponies which he offered to give the officers on hire, and a bare-footed boy named Robert Smith, son of Andrew Smith, retired shipmaster, was sent off to act as guide to the strangers.

"The Standing Stones having been visited, the officers then crossed over to the parish churchyard where they spent some time trying to decipher and translate the Latin inscriptions on the tombstones. They were not very successful in this work, however, and their barefooted guide, who was only about fifteen years of age, was rather horrified to find that the officers in the Navy stumbled in translating phrases which to him had no difficulty. At last he offered to assist them, and caused quite a sensation amongst the strangers by rendering the Latin into English with a freedom that showed he had a good grasp of the language.

"The Admiral (I have been unable to get his name) at once took a liking to the uncouth lad, and on the return journey to Kirkwall made a companion of him. Upon examining the youth, he found that he had got a good sound education, and was specially well up in navigation and languages.

"Subsequently, the Admiral called on Smith's father, told him his boy was far too smart to be wasting his time in Kirkwall, and offered to take him on board his ship and to treat him as if he were his own son.

"Young Smith urged his father to close with the handsome offer, which he at length did.

"Two days afterwards, Robert Smith was installed in the Admiral's cabin as his private secretary. He did not take to life at sea, however, and a few years later, by the influence of the Admiral, he got into the Civil Service.

"He now showed such ability in the discharge of his duties, that his promotion was rapid, and he finished his career as British Consul at Rome."

Another well-known farmer from the West Mainland said he would give a short sketch of Mansie of Beglow.

MANSIE OF BEGLOW

"Mansie," said he, "was a Birsay character, well known
in his day. One who knew him well says she 'Never
kent him speakin' lees or evil o' onybody'; but all the same he
delighted to air the fictions of his imagination. He was a
romancer before the age of cheap books or periodic literature,
else he might have written his novels after the manner of
Marryat. But times were unfavourable, likewise circumstances.
'Chill penury repressed his noble rage,' and thus he was but a
romancer in words—an oral novelist—his audience, any
neighbour who cared to listen to 'his marvellous stories happ'd
by land or sea,' or perhaps the herd-boys who followed their
calling on the banks of the Burn o' Kerse, which flowed below
the house and croft of Beglow.

"Mansie, like Malcolm and a few other Orcadians, was of
a martial spirit, and shared in 'the emotions of the spirit-
stirring time' in which he lived. He used to say that he had
been enlisted twice, and his detractors replied that if he had
gone to the Army a third time he would have been hung.

"When setting forth his war-like exploits he has been heard
to relate that in some south-country ports he saw men enlisting
on one side of a warship, going away for a little, and then
returning to the other side, where they again joined the service,
thus obtaining two bounties! He asserted that he had been at
'the taakin' o' the Rock' (Gibraltar). A neighbour on one
occasion was cruel enough to point out to Mansie that that
event took place before he was born, which at length caused
the old romancer to lay aside that particular fiction.

"Mansie claimed that he had been in the 'Nor-Wast,' where
he had 'shafted his nieve in the face of Wilson, a gigantic
governor who lived there, and threatened to bane-briss him.'
When he was in those cold regions he declared he 'saw ae man
knock aff another man's heid, but he just clapped hid on again.
Hid happened, however, to be put on the wrang way—the
face ahint—but railly he lived a good while after hid.'

"His naval exploits, as set forth by himself, were rather
startling. 'Oor ship,' said he, 'was engaged in action ae day,

when a ball tore a piece oot o' the side o' my waistcoat, and anither carried off the croon o' my hat. Ay, boy,' he would add in telling his story, 'there were hard clods fleein' then. This is the sober truth.'

"Alas, like Sir Walter Scott, a physical infirmity incapacitated him from serving. He had a weak arm, and thus he could not, save in imagination, fight 'for George the Third and glory.' He could not indulge in

> 'His set intent and purpose stony
> To 'list and fight for George,
> And make minced meat of Bony.'

"When the present Mr Spence of Overbist, Birsay, was a young lad out on the hill 'flaying moor,' Beglow, who was passing on his way home from Evie, stopped and told the youngster that he was 'knivellin' i' the heid o' his grandmither.'

"Times must have been good at the whale fishing when Mansie made his voyage to the 'Straits,' as witness the following story told by himself:—'Ae time I wur at the Straits we hed a great fishing. I wur three days i' the hould mither naked, bailing ap oil. Everything was fill o' oil, even the captain's buits, they wur fill! I had three guineas an' a guinea that year'—that is, three certain and one for each fish or number of fish caught.

"Another time Mansie was out shooting along the Loch of Beaquoy, when, according to his own account, he shot—I forget how many—moor-hens, and having forgot the ramrod, he fired it off at the same time. But hear his own words:— 'The ramrod gaed in the loch, an' speeted ap three trouts. An' wi' the force the gun gaed aff, I fell back ower on a hare, and killed her, too!'

"Another time he was pursued in the quaking bog of Clumpsmoss by the bull of Eastabist. But Mansie was not, of course, to be outdone by 'nowte bestial.' He dodged the bull until he got one of the 'eyes'—that is, open holes filled with mud and water—between him and the bull. The bull then charged at Mansie, fell in the 'eye,' Mansie, of course, coming away victorious. But the mad animal sank to rise no more; and such was his fury that, according to Mansie's report of the campaign, 'he heard him boglan till the last point o' the tail gaed oot o' sight!'

"Poor Beglow has now been asleep for many years in the bosom of his 'Grandmither' Earth, but it will be long before he is forgotten in his native parish. His anecdotes are repeated still, and if any one in Birsay is given to 'aarling,' he is pretty certain to receive the title of 'Beglow'."

The old farmer who told those interesting stories about George Taylor and the Cummings then said he had heard an old tradition worth repeating about Brown o' Hackland.

BROWN O' HACKLAND

"In the days when Earl Patrick Stewart held sway in Orkney, feats of strength were the great pastime of the people. When the Earl was in residence at the Birsay Palace, his retainers, on high holidays, gathered out on the green fronting his mansions and engaged in athletic sports. On those occasions the natives were allowed to look on, but they were never asked to take part in any of the games.

"One day the Earl's followers were thus engaged, and amongst the amusements indulged in was putting the stone. Such an ovation was given to the victor, that one of the onlookers offered to produce two men in the parish, either of whom would throw the stone further than had been done that day.

"This statement was treated with derision by the 'ferry-loupers,' and they demanded that the names of these native champions should be given. Louttit of Nettletar and Brown o' Hackland were the names of the chosen men.

"During the hub-hub which ensued, Earl Patrick came on the scene himself and ordered a messenger to be at once sent off on horseback to bring the nearest man, who was Brown o' Hackland. When the champion was found, he was engaged winnowing. He told the messenger to return, and that he would follow on foot when he got through with his job.

"Brown was not only strong of arm, but swift of limb, and he caused some little excitement at the Palace by arriving there as quickly as the man on horseback, though he managed this by crossing fields and leaping fences.

"At the first throw Brown put the stone a yard or two further than any of the Earl's retainers had been able to do— a feat which was rewarded with rounds of cheering by the admiring natives. None of the Earl's men could be induced to try and beat such a throw, whereupon Brown was asked if he could put the stone further, and if so, how far. He replied that he would show them how far he could really put it if the Earl would free him from any damage that might be done. Upon getting this assurance he sent the stone forward with such force that it went right through one of the windows of the Palace, destroying goods inside to the value of several pounds. The fact that this story has been handed down from generation to generation, for hundreds of years, shows how proud the natives were of Brown o' Hackland and his big throw."

"That reminds me," said the West Mainland farmer, "of the story of Magnus Johnston of Overbist, Birsay".

MAGNUS JOHNSTON OF OVERBIST, BIRSAY

"When Magnus Johnston occupied the farm of Overbist, Birsay (about one hundred years ago), the family was rather unfortunate, and one of his sons disappeared in a most mysterious way. This son was the teacher and precentor at Evie, and one day he crossed over to Hundland, Birsay, to see a friend. He admired some books, played a tune or two on a fiddle, and then said he was going out for a short walk. He never returned.

"A most careful search was made for him in all directions, but no trace of him could be got. Days lengthened into weeks, and though the search was unflaggingly kept up, nothing could be learned regarding the fate of the missing man.

"At length Magnus Spence of Skelday had a most marvellous dream, in which he saw and conversed with the long-lost teacher and precentor. Spence demanded that

Johnston should tell him why he remained away from his friends and where he might now be found. To the first question Johnston gave no reply, but said his body was lying so many fathoms deep off the Evie coast.

"This strange dream was repeated from mouth to mouth all over the parish, and such credence was given to it that the search for the missing man was at once given up.

"Another peculiar occurrence in connection with the disappearance of the man was then made public. One day Johnston's mother and aunt had been seen coming along the hill-dyke, from the westward, by the missing man's father. When the two women were some distance from the house, the father saw a third person join them, whom he by-and-by recognised as his lost son.

"Then the women came up to Overbist, they were alone, and they stoutly declared that they had never seen a third person. They also reported that they had been unable to get any news of the son. 'And there never will be any,' was the reply of the father, for he was convinced that he had just seen the young man's 'gonfor' or ghost.

"Now for the sequel. Some years afterwards, when one or two antiquarians were digging in the Knowe of Burgar, Evie, they came upon the skeleton of a human body. There were sufficient indications to prove that the corpse had not been there many years, but no residenter in the parish could remember a burial at that particular place.

"Five years later, a death-bed confession made by a farmer in Rousay, threw considerable light on the strange transaction. The story of the Rousay man was to the effect that he had found the body of Johnston on the shore at Evie; that he had taken a watch and five pounds off it, and that to keep his crime from being detected, he had hidden the remains in the Knowe of Burgar.

"Whatever the rising generation may think of the dream, and the 'gonfor,' there can be no question but that those who took part in the search believed implicitly in both, and the finding of the body, followed by the confession of the Rousay man, at least showed that Johnston had been in the sea off the Evie coast.

"I would like now," continued the West Mainland farmer, "when I am at it, to give you a bit of traditionary lore regarding Sir William Ballantine and Spence of Kirbuster".

SIR WILLIAM BALLANTINE AND SPENCE OF KIRBUSTER

"Sir William Ballantine of Stenness was famous in his day as a swordsman, and for having the stoutest wife in the county. It is related of his good lady that she once went to a feast in a small cothouse in Evie, where she had a name-son. The door was so narrow that it was with difficulty she got into the house, and after the dinner was over the jambs had to be taken away before she could get out!

"Her husband, Sir William Ballantine, or, as he was more familiarly known, 'Stennis,' once did a good turn to the people of Orkney. A swaggering bully had come to the county, and had challenged any man in the place to engage in a duel with him— the weapons to be swords.

"Stennis came forward as the champion for Orkney, and he handled the sword with such effect that he easily conquered the 'ferry-louper.' This victory was so popular with the Kirkwall gentry that they wanted to redeem Stennis' estates which were then sunk in debt. But he was too haughty and proud to receive any such help as an acknowledgement of his prowess.

"Spence of Kirbuster, thinking that too much was being made of the swordsmanship of Stennis, challenged that champion to combat in Broad Street, Kirkwall. The challenge was promptly accepted.

"Before the fight came off, Kirbuster asked his aunt to make his 'dead sark,' as he was afraid he would be killed. The probability is that Kirbuster had sent out the challenge when he was in his cups, and that when in his sober senses he began to repent his rash conduct. However, it turned out that he had little reason to fear, for he succeeded in disarming Stennis, and threw his sword on the top of the 'Towbuith.'

"The version of this duel, as given by the Spences, is as

follows:—When Kirbuster spoke to his aunt about his 'dead sark' he was merely joking. She told him to stop at home, and not to go to the place of meeting. He, however, scoffed at such a proposal. The honour of the duellist and the Spences was at stake. After he had fenced with Stennis for some time, for the purpose of showing what he could do, he made a 'canny' stroke, neatly carving off one of the wrist-buttons of his opponent's shirt. He then told Stennis to look out, as he might take off the neck button next. After this he disarmed Stennis.

"Poor Kirbuster, instead of getting his debt paid in acknowledgement of his prowess, had his property seized by 'the Scotch Earl' for a debt of £60."

"Talking about the West Mainland people," said a traveller, "recalls to mind the case of George Mowat, of Eastabist, Birsay".

George Mowat, of Eastabist, Birsay

"A sad story is told of this young man. He was apprenticed as a sailor, and his qualities as a seaman were so pronounced that, when quite a lad, he was appointed mate. Shortly after this, however, his ship was lost in Eynhallow Sound, and the whole crew went down with it, excepting one boy.

"It seems that there were some lady passengers on board the vessel, and George Mowat had fallen in love with one of them. If he had cared for his own life only, he could easily have reached the shore, as he was an expert swimmer. But he tried to rescue his sweetheart, and other ladies having also clung to him, the whole sank.

"The disaster took place so close to the shore that the people on Eynhallow might without much difficulty have rescued the crew and passengers by throwing out ropes to them, but they were too much occupied in endeavouring to secure the cargo for their own use to give any aid to the drowning sailors and passengers.

"Two explanations may be given of this heartless conduct. There was the old superstitious fear that if help were given to drowning people it brought disease and disaster to the succourers; and it has also to be remembered that the event occurred at a time when food was so scarce in the county that the shores were divided amongst the inhabitants that they might gather the ebb-meat and dulse at low water, and thus be saved from starvation.

"Those bodies which came ashore at Eynhallow from the wreck were promptly stripped, even the ladies' silk dresses being wrenched away from the waist.

"Afterwards the bodies were conveyed across the Sound and buried in a group in Evie churchyard—the place being still pointed out there. George Mowat's father, however, spent a barrel of oil in getting his son's body exhumed and transferred to the burying-ground at Birsay.

"I may add that a curious story is told about this George Mowat's brother. He also was a sailor, and one day when he was passing through the streets of Liverpool he was accosted by a woman, who desired him to go into a house near by. Curious to know what was in the wind, he went. No sooner had his fair companion got him in, however, then she tried to leave the house, endeavouring to lock the

door behind her. John Mowat did not like the look that matters had now assumed. He said he was quite agreeable to wait the return of the woman if she desired to make any message, but he absolutely refused to allow the door to be locked on him.

"His fair companion had to accept those terms, and when she left him alone he began examining the room. To his horror he found a man's body stowed away in a corner. This circumstance was so suspicious that he thought it was now time to be moving. As he was hurrying up the street, he saw the woman walking with a policeman, and, as he passed, he heard her say—'I left him in the house.'

"This remark led him to believe that the woman wished to saddle the crime upon him, but he never heard anything further of the affair, though he felt grateful that he had got so easily out of what might have been a nasty scrape."

"Now," said the West Mainland farmer, "I will give you my last story—and it is regarding a character whom none of you ever saw, but with whose name you must all be familiar—I refer to Mansie o' Harra".

MANSIE O' HARRA

"There can be no question about Mansie's originality, and the present lairds of Harray talk as familiarly about the old man as if they had all known him, yet he must have been called to his rest before most of them were born. Mansie was brimful of mother-wit. At church or at market, whenever he met his neighbours, he had something droll to say, and the fact that some of the stories told regarding him have been handed down through several generations, speaks volumes for the impression which his wit made upon contemporaries.

"It is told of Mansie that on one occasion he went to Stromness to sell a cow. His wife, Betty, to make sure that she got the money, accompanied her husband to the market. By and by the animal was sold — the price fixed upon being four guineas. Betty heard the bargain struck, so that there seemed but little chance of Mansie getting as much off the transaction as would 'wet his whistle.' Mansie, however, was too resourceful to be done out of his dram. Taking the dealer aside, he whispered in the ear of that worthy that Betty could not distinguish the difference between a guinea note and a pound note, and that it would suit him best to have payment made in paper of the latter denomination. When he got the four pound notes, Betty at once pounced upon them and made off to put them out of the reach of her husband. 'Man,' said Mansie to the dealer, 'isn't that grand. The coast is clear, so we'll awa' doon to the public and melt the four shillings. Betty will get a bonnie surprise when she meets me roarin' fu'!'

"Mansie had a son who was a seaman on board a Davis Strait whale-fishing ship. On one occasion this vessel put into Stromness, and on the news reaching Harray, Mansie travelled into town in order to see his son. On reaching Stromness he procured a small boat and pulled off to the vessel. Getting alongside he hailed the ship, when a man looked over the rail and asked what he wanted. 'O', replied Mansie, 'ye needna been in sic a hurry, and com'd up through the lum! Ye could hae opened the door; but I cam' tae speer for me son.' It was at once seen that Mansie was a character, so that he was taken on board, and was prevailed upon to stay till next morning. During the night a strong gale arose, which made the ship roll and pitch rather heavily. In the morning Mansie came on deck, and was walking backwards and forwards, when he espied two or three small boats fastened astern. 'Weel, weel,' said he, 'it's nae winder the puir cratur' was in pain, an' keeked aboot in the nicht as she did. See whit she has calved!'

"On another occasion Mansie was in Stromness with his old mare. On leaving the town he noticed some fishermen putting boiling tar on their boat. Mansie enquired what they were doing that for, and was told that it was to make the boat 'run.' 'I wish ye wid only pit some o't on me auld mare, an' see if hid widna' mak' her rin,' said Mansie. One of the men then dipped the 'mop' in the boiling tar, and dashed it on the mare, when the animal immediately bolted, throwing Mansie into the ditch. Mansie had got a severe shaking by the fall, and was not in the best of humour when he arose. After travelling along the road for some distance he came upon his old mare lying dead on the roadside—her teeth being tightly closed and her lips slightly open. On seeing this, Mansie apparently thought the mare was laughing at him, for he lifted his stick and belaboured the dead animal, at the same time exclaiming: 'Ah, ye auld jade, will ye lie there an' laugh at me noo, after pitchin' me in the ditch an' trying to kill me?'

"The most humourous stories regarding Mansie, however, are those which are best forgotten, and I am not going to give any of these. Those which I have just been relating will suffice to show, in a general way, what sort of man he was."

By the time all the foregoing stories had been discussed, bed-time had arrived, and though the gale continued unabated, the company retired to rest in the best of spirits, feeling they had spent a very enjoyable evening.

One winter night some neighbours gathered at Claybraes, in the East Mainland; and, as usually happens on such occasions, they began to exchange reminiscences of the past. Old Tammie Tait the tailor, who is famed as a story-teller, commenced the proceedings by giving a biographical sketch of Donald Levach.

DONALD LEVACH

"This worthy," said Tammie, "was not born in Orkney. He was well known throughout the islands, however, and spent the greater part of his life here, so that it may fairly be claimed for him that, if not an Orcadian he was so at least by adoption. Donald was a native of Halkirk, Caithness. When a youth he learned the tailoring trade, but he did not work very long at it, leaving it to become a book-canvasser for the firm of Messrs. Blackie & Son, Glasgow. It was in this capacity, and while he was quite a young man, that he came to Orkney (landing in South Ronaldsay from Huna)— being the pioneer canvasser for the firm of Messrs. Blackie & Son in the county—

and he continued in this employment till he died. He proved a most successful canvasser, and might have been well off had it not been for his one great failing—a love of whisky—for I must admit that he periodically went on the spree. He had in his youth received little or no education, and he used to say that 'the only schoolbook ever bought for Tonald was a Caracher.' But Donald made up his mind to get rid of this disadvantage. He laboured hard to improve himself. He was a great reader, chiefly of standard works, and he closely studied human nature. Having a very retentive memory, he soon gathered a large store of general information.

"Gaelic being his native language, he invariably used T in place of D, P instead of B, etc., at the commencement of words. He was ready-witted, quick in repartee, and his jokes were all original. He had two half-brothers, one a minister the other an hotel-keeper, and he used to say, 'I have two prothers, they both deal with spirits, but it is different kinds—one is trying to save men, the other to destroy them.'

"I once heard him say, in a tailor's shop in School Place, Kirkwall, 'I have a prother ten feet high!' This called forth the sneering comment, 'O, Donald, that will do,' to which Donald replied, 'Well, you are a man that will reason, aren't you? Two halves make whole, don't they?' 'Yes,' admitted his opponent. 'Well, then,' continued Donald, 'I have two half prothers, and I am sure each of them is over five feet high, so that will surely make one prother ten feet high!'

"Donald used to tell with much gusto how he sold a Free Church woman a Bible. Entering the house shortly after the Disruption, the woman was very severe in her animadversions on the Established Church, and could talk of nothing but the evil deeds of the Intrusionists. At length Donald said, 'My good woman, would you buy a Free Kirk Bible?' Of course she would. So Donald sold her a Bible, and on leaving her told her to be sure and read very carefully I Cor., xiii, and advised her to try to live up to it.

"One J—— M—— had subscribed for a commentary on the Bible, and after taking a few of the parts, wished to get rid of his obligation. He therefore offered to sell Donald the parts cheap. Donald, however, did not look with favour at the proposal. Addressing the young man, he said, 'John, have you ever read your Pible?' 'A little,' was the reply. 'Well,' continued Donald, 'have you ever found the passage, 'Puy the truth, and sell it not?' 'I think not,' said John. 'Then go home and read till you find it, and act up to it?' was Donald's advice.

"Once he was in a shop in Stromness rather the worse of whisky, when an elder of one of the churches came in. Donald turned to him and said, 'Will you puy a pook?' 'What are you selling—spectacles?' queried the elder. "Pooks," cried Donald; the Pible—the best of pooks.' 'I consider that a man who sells the Bible,' said the elder, 'ought to be a decent, respectable party, and not one who makes a fool of himself with whisky,' to which Donald promptly replied, 'Do you ever read your Pible?' 'Yes,' said the elder. 'Well,' continued Donald, with scathing indignation, 'did you ever read that among the Jews the raven was counted an unclean bird, and yet she fed the holy prophet Elijah?'

"Once he was in Mr Leith's tailor shop in St Margaret's Hope, when the Rev. Mr Edgar, then U.P. minister of South Ronaldsay, entered and commenced to lecture him on the evils of using intoxicating liquor. Donald mildly suggested that the parson would be as well employed looking after some of his own members. But the minister still continuing his well-meant remonstrances, Donald exclaimed, 'Do you see Gaan Petrie's shed out there?' pointing to a boat-carpenter's shop; 'your church is just like that shed—open at both ends—ready to receive anything that comes in, but they can as easily get out by the other end.'

"One day a former postmaster of Kirkwall and another gentleman were standing in front of the Post Office, when they saw Donald strolling up the street. Thinking to have some sport at the expense of the Highlandman, they waited till he came up. The postmaster then accosted him. 'Well, Donald, we were disputing, and thought perhaps you could set us right. You know that in Orkney the United Presbyterian denomination is predominant. Now, Caithness is a much larger county than Orkney. How is it that in all Caithness there is only one small U.P. congregation?' Donald placed his finger on the side of his nose, as he was in the habit of doing when studying and replied, 'Well, sir, there are not so many tammed scoondrals in the whole County of Caithness as would make one fairsized U.P. congregation!' His interrogator was so nonplussed that he bolted into the Post Office, leaving Donald and the other gentleman standing in the middle of the street, while the bystanders were convulsed with laughter.

"I have already indicated that Donald was a little too fond of whisky. He knew his weakness, and sometimes made strenuous efforts to resist the temptation—only one of which I shall relate. Having been on the spree in Stromness, he left and proceeded to a house outside the town, where he stopped till he got sober. At last he set out for Kirkwall, to reach which he would naturally have to pass through Finstown, where there was at that time at least one public house and one shebeen right in his road. Donald, knowing his weakness, was afraid to risk the temptation, there being, as he used to say, 'lions in the way'; so he went up through Germiston, Stenness, crossed the hill of Heddle, came down near the old Firth Manse, took the old Stromness road, and thus got into Kirkwall without encountering 'the lions' he was afraid to face. He was strictly honest and very conscientious. Often when drinking, after his money ran out, he would borrow from anyone who would lend him, and when he could get no more, he would go to the publicans, who rarely refused to give him liquor on 'tick'. As soon as he got sober and commenced to work, the first money he earned went to pay the debts thus contracted, he, often denying himself the necessaries of life to get this accomplished. I used to say to him that I did not consider he had any right, legal or moral, to refund those men who sold him liquor without money when they saw the state he was in, as they were conferring no favour on him; but his answer always was, 'all true; but I went into them—they did not come out to me'."

John Anderson, a canny-going old farmer, over whose head some four-score summers had passed, said he would tell them the story of Geordie Gaudie.

GEORDIE GAUDIE

He said he had often heard old people tell it, but the best account he knew of was that of Mr Duncan McLean, a native of Kirkwall, who had been in the Navy, and who had risen to the proud position of being editor of the *Boston Traveller.*

"Most of you know that Geordie Gaudie was a noted tramp seventy years ago. He was about five feet eight inches high, weighed at least two hundred pounds, was well-proportioned, with red hair sprinkled with grey bushy whiskers and beard, had an open, manly caste of countenance, and large, expressive blue eyes. In his youth he must have been one of the best-looking men of his day. He wore a Scotch cap, a brown monkey jacket, and was trim in his rig throughout.

"He wandered aimlessly over the islands, rarely remaining more than a day in one place. Occasionally he turned up in Kirkwall, took a look at the shipping, visited the Auld Kirk, lingered lovingly in the graveyard, and among the ruins of the Earl's Palace. The boys, who were always on hand for a 'lark' with odd characters, rarely troubled him, for he was genial and kind, and when spoken to answered courteously, but briefly, for he was a man of few words. The boys having learned that he detested the sight of money, especially silver coins, occasionally offered him a sixpence; then he sprang at them in wrath, and they soon disappeared.

"He was a native of North Ronaldsay, where he had a brother and a sister, well-to-do folks, with whom he lived when out of kelter, and who were very kind to him, for they had shared his prosperity when in luck. When a boy he entered the Royal Navy, at a time when 'gold chains and wooden legs' were served out; the gold to the officers, the wood to the shellbacks. Shortly after the peace of 1815 he returned to Orkney and became a wanderer, but even his brother and sister knew not why.

"Many years afterwards, when serving in the Navy myself, I became shipmate with a man who knew him well in his prime, then one of the most dashing, daring, and handsome men

afloat. He had served with Nelson in the battle of St Vincent, at the Nile, Copenhagen and Trafalgar, and on board the Pallas frigate, under Lord Cochrane, when he burned the French fleet in Basque Roads. Most of the time he was a quartermaster, belonged to Nelson's barge, and had been complimented by Lady Hamilton as the finest-looking fellow in the great Admiral's barge. Nelson, himself a rare specimen of manly beauty, had his barge and gig manned with the best-looking men in his ship.

"Geordie, having an excellent character, received employment in Portsmouth dockyard, which assured him a good living while able to work, and a pension when invalided. He had been lucky in prize-money and saving of his wages, so that he had over one thousand pounds on hand when he left the sea. His life, for a plain, unlettered man, had thus far been a complete success; he knew his duty and did it man-fashion. The old saying, 'Never call a man lucky until he is under ground,' was painfully illustrated in his case. Unfortunately he fell in love with a beautiful girl (all bad girls are beautiful, according to the novelists, who know everything), and Geordie's turned out one of the number. She was the daughter of a shipmate, pious after a fashion, and bore an unblemished character. They were married and lived lovingly together for a whole year, until she had obtained control of his money, then she disappeared, money and all. He did not make any outcry, but sold his furniture, paid what little he owed resigned his place at the dockyard, packed up his clothes, and came to the home of his brother and sister, where he left his chest and clothing, and some fifty pounds in money obtained from the sale of his furniture and the last instalment of his wages. He remained about a week at home, and then took to wandering. Wherever he brought up at night he was kindly received and hospitably entertained. He seemed to know by instinct where to go. During the warm months of summer he slept in the fields, and was sure to receive something to eat when he was hungry. When the whalemen came to Stromness to complete their crews, he boarded them, had a draw of the clay and a glass or two of grog, for he seemed to love the men of the sea, and little children, though he was never seen to smile. No doubt regarding money as the cause of his bad luck, he literally abhorred the very sight of it. When his clothes were worn out, and he felt that he needed to refit ship, he came home, but never remained longer than a few days. I think he was still wandering in 1828 when I left Kirkwall; but he is no doubt now in heaven, for the last old shellback who was sent to the other place could not get in; it was chock full, and land sinners were sitting with their legs out of the windows. Like an omnibus, in which there is always room for 'one more,' it is to be hoped that this faithless rib is that one."

Mansie Bews said he would like to tell them about the greatest town-crier and town-piper that Kirkwall ever had—Jamie Wallace.

JAMIE WALLACE

"Those who knew this famous town-crier," said Mansie, "say that he had a strong, clear, trumpet-like voice, and made his announcements with so much lung power that he could be heard from a great distance. His worst fault was that he took a dram, and on these occasions he was not very choice in his language. But with all his faults in these respects, he seems to have been a great favourite with the inhabitants. He was the last official piper of Kirkwall, and every morning for many years, he, with the stirring strains of his pipes, called from their slumber the horny-handed sons of toil. One morning, however, the pipes were silent, and the news spread that Wallace had fallen from a cart near New England the previous evening, and had broken his neck. The loss of the piper was felt to be a great one, and many times were the Council coaxed to fill up the vacant office. The municipal rulers, however, were obdurate, and no successor was appointed; but Wallace is embalmed in the memory of many as 'a piper of renown'."

Another member of the company, old Donald MacLean, said—

"This honest man, from the time I first knew him until I left Kirkwall, every morning, except Sunday, played his pipes through the main street. One morning he would begin at the upper end, and the next at the quay, so that all should have their fair share of his music, which was designed to call the toilers to work. He was not only a talented player but a man of spiritual endowments. He was in open communication with ghosts long before the 'Rochester-Knockings' of New York, but never made merchandize of his gifts. At will he could 'call up spirits from the vasty deep,' and they would come and tell him all he wished to know. I think he also rang the town bell nightly at eight o'clock. It was only when the 'cockles of his heart' were warm with whisky, and a very little water, for the water at that time was not very good, that he was eloquent about the glories of the good place, condition of their denizens . . . He prided himself on his descent from the heroic Wallace, and though his occupation was humble, he said the name should never be dishonoured in his person.

"A local poet and admirer of Jamie Wallace wrote the following elegy on him:—

"Kirkwallians, list' to what I tell;
  He's gone, whose notes awoke the morn,
  He's gone from you, who bore the bell;
  And to his narrow house he's borne.

"St. Magnus still may tell the time,
  But he'll not now prolong the chime;
  No more will Jamie take his round;
  For low he lies beneath the ground.

"He had his faults, but let them rest;
  Faults stick to characters the best;
  Of this I'm sure that Kirkwall town
  Has lost a Piper of renown."